RIDING THE STORM

To Mary, my wife, my best friend.

Riding the Storm

BARRY KISSELL

KINGSWAY PUBLICATIONS
EASTBOURNE

First published 2000

ISBN 0 85476 865 3

Published by
KINGSWAY PUBLICATIONS
Lottbridge Drove, Eastbourne, BN23 6NT, England.
E-mail: books@kingsway.co.uk

Designed and produced for the publishers by
Bookprint Creative Services, P.O. Box 827, BN21 3YJ, England.
Printed in Great Britain.

Contents

Preface

When I was first asked to write this testimony I hesitated for a number of reasons. The first was that I did not want to write a book about myself, but rather about Jesus Christ and the ways in which he is able through his Spirit to help those who ask him. I also realized that if this book was to be an encouragement to others I would need to be vulnerable and completely honest and open with my thoughts and emotions. This inevitably meant that what I wrote could be misconstrued by others, as it is a reflection of how I saw and interpreted situations, which may not be as others did. I have considered this carefully and hope readers will accept it in the spirit in which I have sought to write.

Everything that has happened to Mary and me has been intertwined with the lives of our own family and that of the Muffins. Jonathan, Timothy and Noonie have always been there to comfort and encourage us, especially when the storm was at its height. The Muffins – Dylan, Natasha, Bruce and Bianca – whom we had the privilege of welcoming into our family and home, have shown in their lives the power of Jesus to restore from extreme trauma.

During our time in New Zealand many people corresponded with us through letters, cards, tapes, drawings and gifts of one sort or another. Many telephoned regularly with words of comfort and support. The people of St Andrew's, Chorleywood, were always there for us and in practical ways showed great love and kindness. For this and all the prayers offered I shall for ever be grateful.

I wish to thank the staff at Palmerston North Hospital, New Zealand. Especially Mr McCormick, whose skill put my neck together again, and his registrars Rob and Gordon, who became my friends. And to Joy my staff nurse and to Anna the ward sister and her great team of encouragers.

I am grateful to Frazer, Nigel and Andy, leaders of the local community church, who with their fellowship supplied our every need, even down to taking me to a rugby match in a wheelchair and giving Mary the use of a car with petrol coupons.

Finally I want to acknowledge my appreciation to my editors Chris and Alison Walley. Their professionalism and sense of fun made the rewrites palatable.

Barry Kissell

1

Storm Warnings

We like predictability.

Even Christians – who ought to know better – want to have the future mapped out for them. We plan our destinations in life, plot the smoothest course to them, and set off, expecting plain sailing. But God has his own agenda.

My story is how God suddenly, unexpectedly and painfully intervened in my own life and savagely threw me off the course I had plotted for myself. After three years of tossing and shaking, I now see in what happened that the Holy Spirit was working radically and breaking down the hidden deep strongholds of pride in my ministry.

The first hint of the storm ahead came from the Kansas City prophets.

I had initially been exposed to the ministry of prophets in the early 70s when, as a young Anglican curate, I did a tour of the Church of North India with Michael Harper. Together we spoke at a leaders' conference at Bangalore. The diocese there had just had a visit from an African prophet and a remark by the bishop about this made an indelible imprint on my mind. He said that there was nothing like a visit of a prophet who genuinely heard the voice of God, to sort out the spiritual and moral life of a diocese. The illustrations he gave made my hair stand on end. Until then my understanding of the ministry of contemporary prophets had been of mature Christian leaders who read *The Times* or *The Daily Telegraph* and commented on the national and international news from a Christian perspective. My views began to change.

Later in my ministry I came to know John Wimber, founder of the Vineyard churches; we first met in 1981 when he came to St Andrew's, Chorleywood, where I was on the staff. On a subsequent visit he spoke at a day for leaders and after his talk he invited the Holy Spirit to minister. Almost immediately, John came and prayed over me, and what he said to me obviously came from a revelation that the Spirit had given him. Much later he told me that after that meeting he had prayed for me every day.

John invited me to visit him in California on a number of occasions, always insisting that he would pay the cost. Such a visit, he said, would enable us to get to know each other better. We could go fishing together. Once, after a tour in New Zealand, I even arranged a stop-off in Los Angeles, but circumstances prevented us from meeting.

On the 11th July 1990, John was in London leading a conference at Holy Trinity Brompton, a prominent Anglican church. With him were a group of men who had become known as the Kansas City prophets, around whose ministry a good deal of controversy had become attached. Encouraged by what I knew of John's personal integrity, I went to the conference with my wife Mary.

There Mary and I were invited with other leaders to a private meeting with the prophets in the church crypt. Entering the room, we found three of them seated together behind a table. We were asked to sit facing them. As we sat down, the leader, Bob Jones, said in a friendly American drawl, 'It's sure good to see you again. Just remind me, where did we last meet?'

Surprised, I replied, 'We have never met.'

Apparently oblivious to what I had just said, he continued, 'Have you been to Kansas City?'

'No,' I answered.

'Then have I ever spoken in your church?'

'No,' I repeated emphatically, feeling rather embarrassed.

In apparent bewilderment Bob stared at me. 'I am confused because I seem to know you very well.'

I began to wonder whether it had been such a good idea to have accepted the invitation to the meeting. I tried to ease his confusion. 'The first time I saw you was this morning as I arrived at the conference. We walked together through the same door. A colleague said to me, "That is Bob Jones from Kansas City."'

'I've got it,' Bob said suddenly, with apparent relief. 'We've been in London for two nights and each night I have seen you in my dreams, and this is what I saw.'

What happened in the next few minutes was overwhelming. For many years I have kept a diary in which I have recorded what to me have been significant events. In it I have included what I have felt to be revelations from God and the details of visions, dreams and words that have been given to me. In many ways this private diary has charted my spiritual pilgrimage. And as Bob spoke it was as if he had had access to this.

I started to weep as he spoke of my past in detail, highlighting disappointments and sorrows. He described clearly the Christian ministry I had been involved in and the ways in which he saw God developing this. Before the other prophets spoke over me Bob ended with these words: 'The days are coming when the Lord will take from you everything you have built up and relied upon.'

At the time these sobering words made no sense.

After Bob had spoken with a similar extraordinary accuracy over Mary we decided to leave the conference. Stunned, we walked weeping quietly down to the Serpentine. There under the warmth of the bright sun we sat together on the grass. For some time neither of us spoke and then slowly we began to reminisce together on what we had heard. Although much of what Bob had said had been encouraging and affirming, his final words resounded in my mind like a solemn bell. Although I could not express it in words, even to Mary, I knew deep down, despite the sunlight shining on us, that I was about to sail into uncharted waters with God. Intuitively I sensed that I would be 'riding the storm'. But I never dreamed how violent and life-threatening the winds and waves would be.

In the busy months that followed, I occasionally reread Bob's prophetic words for us that I had recorded in my diary, but slowly their impact faded.

The next warning came on the 3rd May 1994. I had been invited by Chris Wood, the vicar of Holy Trinity, Parr Mount, to speak at a celebration he was hosting for the churches in the St Helen's area of Liverpool. Some years before, I had led a Faith Sharing Team to this church for a week of meetings in people's homes to which seekers after God had been invited. In addition to a number of people coming to find a personal faith in Jesus Christ, there had been healings and many manifestations of the Holy Spirit, including prophetic utterances.

Returning was a great encouragement. The renovated church was full and there was a great sense of expectation as a band led the worship and a number of people shared how Jesus was helping them in their lives. I spoke and then there was a time of ministry in the power of the Holy Spirit. As the meeting was concluding, Chris came over with a lady called Irene, who asked whether she could speak to me privately. As we made our way to an adjacent room, Chris told me that

Irene was a prophetess and, although a relatively young Christian, had an impressive track record for accuracy.

We sat down together and Irene began, 'As you were speaking tonight, I saw you sinking up to your neck in water. It appeared as if you were drowning. I sensed the enemy was pulling you down. Then in the vision I saw the Lord's hand reaching down and pulling you up. But you must cry to the Lord.'

Irene kept emphasizing the need to 'cry to the Lord'. Then she paused for a moment and said, 'It's 2 Samuel chapter 22, verse 17.'

Chris explained that usually when Irene had a prophetic revelation she would quote a scripture at random. At that stage of her Christian life Irene would probably never have read the scripture she was quoting, especially if it happened to be in the depths of the Old Testament.

I opened my Bible and found the verse. It read, 'He reached down from on high and took hold of me; he drew me out of deep waters.'

As the words registered, my eyes glanced up the page, trying to find the context of the words. New words struck me: 'The waves of death swirled about me; the torrents of destruction overwhelmed me. The cords of the grave coiled around me; the snares of death confronted me. In my distress, I called out to the LORD; I called out to my God. From his temple he heard my voice; my cry came to his ears' (2 Samuel 22:5–7).

In hindsight, it was another warning. However, at the time I was very busy and fulfilled, and Irene's prophecy seemed to have little relevance. I decided that the message was a prediction of a period of storms in my ministry when I would need to rely more on the Lord.

Would it have helped if I had correctly interpreted the danger ahead? Probably not. There are some traumas you can never be adequately prepared for. One consolation that such warning prophecies bring though is the reassuring knowledge that God already knows about such trials and can therefore help you and bring you through.

If over the months that followed I was not concerned by the two prophecies, what did begin to trouble me was the nature of my ministry. I have found that when the Lord wants to speak to me in a direct way through the Scriptures he has a way of highlighting the text almost as if the passage has been underscored with a marking pen. Now, whenever I read the Gospels I was always being drawn to think about an incident involving Jesus and the two brothers, James and John, recorded in chapter 10 of Mark's Gospel.

On this occasion, James and John had come to Jesus with a request. Looking forward to the day when Jesus would come to earth again and establish his kingdom in all its fullness, they requested that when this happened they could sit either side of him. In his reply Jesus asked, 'Can you drink the cup I drink or be baptised with the baptism I am baptised with?' (v. 38). Jesus' question was to do with the suffering and self-denial that lay at the very heart of his life and ministry. Without thought and heedless of the implications of his response, the brothers indicated that they could. Jesus replied that they would indeed share in his cup and baptism.

The word 'meditation' in Hebrew can also mean 'to mutter' and suggests the idea of going over and over a particular point as we let the Holy Spirit direct our thinking. As, over many months, I meditated on this incident in the Gospels, God started to challenge me uncomfortably on areas where in my motivation and ministry I had become proud and self-seeking.

I began to see glaring parallels between James and John and myself. Their desire had been for visibility. After all, you could not have greater cosmic visibility than to appear at the right and left of the Son of God in his glory at the end of time! Allied to the desire for visibility had come a desire for authority and exclusive relationship that went with it. They had wanted a kingdom within the kingdom of Jesus. Gradually and painfully, I began to see that I was like them in my buried desires for prominence and authority.

My ministry had been an undeniable success. I had been the speaker at celebrations in 23 cathedrals and been invited to minister in 25 nations. I had published books and taken part in and presented television programmes. In 1974 I had founded the Faith Sharing Ministry, and through it I had led teams to over a thousand churches and had had opportunities to speak at national and international conferences. When Bishop David Pytches had started the New Wine family conference at the Royal Bath and West Showground at Shepton Mallet in Somerset in 1988, he had invited Mary and me to co-host it with him. Over the years the New Wine conference had become an annual event drawing thousands of people. Soul Survivor, a major national Christian youth movement, had been born out of the young people who gathered at New Wine.

Yet although many people had plainly found aspects of my ministry helpful, I now began to see that there were elements of self-seeking in much of what I had done. I had used these opportunities to build a kingdom within the kingdom.

The problem had grown so subtly. As a young man, I once had a boil under my right arm. I was only aware of it when someone knocked into me; then the pain made me respond angrily. I saw that I had similar symptoms now and that I reacted strongly when 'my' kingdom was threatened. It dawned on me that I had come to refer too much to what I did as '*my* ministry'. I realized that what I did had given me identity and significance, and had helped sustain me.

Coming to terms with truth is often uncomfortable, and facing a truth like this is especially so. When God speaks to me in a challenging way, my first reaction is often to pretend that I am inventing the rebuke. After all, I tell myself, I am busy about God's work. Perhaps I may concede there may have been moments when my motivation has not been correct. These though do not make a major problem; a little confession will put everything right. It was in such a spirit that I initially dealt with the nagging incident with James and John.

That is until I heard Jesus say to me: 'You have made yourself a somebody, but I am making you a nobody. I am preparing you for the harvest.'

Over the months ahead I turned back again and again to the James and John story. I realized that the reason they had to undergo suffering was to enable Jesus to make them into his servants. Jesus had shown them by his example that, although he was the Son of God, he had come to earth to be a servant of men and not to be the one served. The ultimate expression of this would be seen in his giving of his life, the price paid to free men from their prisons. Jesus was showing these young men that it would be his servants who would bring in the harvest. Yet how it applied to me was still unclear.

Our Easter Day Sunday celebrations of the resurrection of Jesus always start just before daybreak on Chorleywood common. The young people from the churches lead worship and together we praise and thank the Lord. The Easter story is read and someone will share a thought about the risen Jesus before we have a simple breaking of bread. The gathering usually finishes when, holding hands and forming an enormous circle, we say a closing prayer together.

As I walked home with others for breakfast from the celebration on Easter Day 1996, I felt I heard the Lord say to me, 'This year will be your last New Wine.' The annual conference where I had spoken to thousands had become a place of great visibility for me. I made the difficult and painful decision to resign as Director.

That summer our last New Wine conference was a fantastic occasion. As I walked off the stage at the conclusion of the final evening, I could feel the tears welling up. For eight wonderful years this had been such a major part of both my own life and ministry and that of Mary. From the conference, we went on holiday in Cornwall, staying in Hayle at the chalet of Alan and Sue Higgins, friends for over 30 years.

Mary and I wanted to spend time together thinking and praying about the future. Both of us felt we were on the verge of new things. I had had the incredible privilege of being on the staff of St Andrew's Church, Chorleywood, for 25 years. Here I had served my second curacy and established the Faith Sharing Ministry. After Bishop David Pytches had retired as Vicar after 19 years, I would lead the church for six months while we awaited the appointment of Mark Stibbe as the new vicar. The plans were for me to be with Mark until he had settled in, then Mary and I would move on to new things. I had seven years to go before I officially retired and I wanted to give those years to the Lord for him to do with me what he wanted and to take me where he chose. Mary too was anticipating change. For 14 years she had been a tutor at a hospice, where she had taught on the care of the dying, but now she planned to retire. Mary is an excellent teacher and writer and with our children having left home, we were looking forward to travelling much more, sharing the teaching and ministry together. There in Cornwall we were able to spend a lot of time together reading the Bible and praying. In our prayers, we recommitted our lives to the Lord and openly gave our futures to him. We wanted him to use us in any way he chose.

The day before our departure, I rose early and stood for a moment at the chalet door, looking out towards the estuary. Suspended above the Hayle River was a glowing, perfect arc of a rainbow that ended in the sea. I called Mary to join me. As we stood together in the early morning we both felt that this was a sign that the Lord was renewing his covenant with us. With great excitement and anticipation about our future, we returned home. We had no idea of the implications of our open offer to serve him in any way he chose. We had no way of knowing what the personal cost would be.

Within days the Lord challenged the validity of our commitment. On the 23rd August 1996 the front door bell rang. Standing with Will Kemp, our youth worker, were four traumatized and frightened young people. A few hours earlier, their father had murdered their mother. Although the family had worshipped at our church some months before, they had since left to join another church. I had never had a conversation with the children – our only contact had been a mutual greeting as they left a service.

We took them in and Mary made them breakfast. As she did, we wondered who I could ask to look after them out of our kind and loving congregation. We soon realized that it would be wrong to split them up. But who could accommodate four young people? Later that day Mary suggested that until other arrangements could be made, they stay with us. Somehow we managed to fit them into our home, but it was quite a squash.

They were still with us six weeks later and I felt it was probably time to make more permanent arrangements. As I discussed this with Mary, she looked at me. 'Barry,' she said, 'I think the Lord is telling me that we should become their foster parents and have them living with us. Permanently.'

I was shaken. For one thing it definitely did not fit in with what I saw as the answer to our recent prayers about our future. Mary and I were not going to be travelling together very far with a traumatized twelve-year-old girl to look after. Anyway, I felt it had been hard enough bringing my own three children through their teenage years. The idea of going through it again with four young people I hardly knew filled me with apprehension. I told Mary that we needed to wait before such a decision was made. Even in the short time they had been with us I had come to love the children, but I didn't see us having a long-term involvement with them. It hardly fitted with our plans. But God overruled me.

Because of the circumstances surrounding the death of the children's mother, we realized that it was going to be a long time before the coroner could release the body. Together we decided to have an initial service of thanksgiving in our church and to follow this up later with a service at the crematorium. At the service of thanksgiving, I saw what an incredible family these children were. Each one wrote an appreciation of their mother's life and read it during the service. Never, it seemed, had their faith in Jesus wavered. During these initial days of loss and trauma, they quietly drew strength from reading the Scriptures and praying. Their mother had been a committed Christian and had obviously imparted to each of her children a deep and real faith. Unknown to us all, this faith was going to be tested yet further. They too were going to be struck by the storm that was soon to break over us.

Finally, the mother's body was released and we were able to prepare for the service at the crematorium. I suggested that the children each write a letter to their mother and say the things they would have wanted to say if they had the chance. We arrived in the chapel of the crematorium and stood together around the coffin. I read a short passage of Scripture on the hope of the resurrection, and said a simple prayer. I then invited the family to place their letters on the coffin and say anything they wanted to. As they were doing this, I heard Jesus speak to me in an audible voice, 'Today I give you this family to parent and care for.'

Tears started to stream down my face and I started to sob deeply. Questions flooded my mind. How could I possibly have the resources for such a task? Could this be part of the Lord's will in response to the recommitment of my life? Yet as I heard the voice of God, I knew that I had to make a response. I sobbed back my answer. 'Yes, Lord, if you will be my helper.'

On the 28th September 1996 I celebrated 25 years of joining the staff of St Andrew's, Chorleywood. The congregation announced that they would like to commemorate the 25 years by paying for Mary and me to go home to my native New Zealand for a three-week holiday. We were thrilled at the opportunity to see family and friends, and to spend time just with each other.

But what were we going to do with our new family? Richard and Ingrid Myers provided the answer. The previous summer we had led a three-month Bible school in Russian Siberia and when planning it I had invited Richard and Ingrid to come as hosts for the duration of the school. It had not been easy for the Russian students, as they were sent out in twos for ten days each. In a culture that was strange to them, all the young leaders had found Richard and Ingrid a constant source of love and encouragement, and although retired themselves I had seen how they related easily to the Russian young people. With that in mind I asked Richard and Ingrid if they would stay in our home and look after our new family for the three weeks we would be away. They immediately committed themselves.

So, early in January 1997, with matters in the church and at home settled, we packed our bags for the trip to New Zealand with great excitement. Things were back on course.

We were unaware that our long-prophesied storm was finally about to break over us.

2
The Waves Break

As Mary and I journeyed halfway around the world to New Zealand, our thoughts and discussions were of the long hot summer days and prolonged balmy evenings that lay ahead. However, the weather we faced on arrival was very different and we found ourselves stepping off the aircraft into the tail end of a cyclone that had recently swept across the Pacific. We dashed from the newly modernized airport at Auckland through torrential rain to the waiting car of our friends Ian and Jane MacCormack, who had travelled up from Tauranga to meet us.

Ian and Jane had stayed with us several times in England when Ian was on a speaking tour. Ian had had an extraordinary encounter with death. He had clinically died as the result of being repeatedly stung by a shoal of poisonous jellyfish while snorkelling off the coast of Mauritius. As he was dying he committed his life to Jesus Christ and had come back to life in a hospital room. Little did I know how closely I was to come to relate to Ian's experience of death and resurrection.

It was still very early in the morning as Mary and I drove north in the car that Ian and Jane had lent us. It was still dark and with the wind and driving rain we both commented how strangely ominous and foreboding everything felt. We stopped for breakfast at a café on the coastal road just south of the thermal pools at Waiwera and from our table we looked out through the rain-lashed windows onto the Hauraki Gulf where the sea was in turmoil. Around us we could hear people in the café discussing the abnormal summer weather and the devastation the cyclone had caused to the East Coast regions.

Over the next few days the weather gradually cleared and the storm gave way to days of sunshine and showers. After ten days of touring the north we moved south to visit my mother, who lived in Feilding, a few miles outside of Palmerston North. Our plans were to stay with her for the last two weeks of our holiday before returning home.

On the morning of the 9th January when Mary awoke, she told me of an intense and unprecedented vision she had had. In her vision, she had felt that she was standing at the foot of a bank of vivid green grass. A sound had got progressively louder and then suddenly a train had appeared thundering down the track. As it passed her along the top of the bank she heard the words, 'Nothing will stop my plans and purposes.' She then became aware of a 'mocking spirit' that diverted her attention for a moment. She watched as the train roared steadily on and the voice of God said again, 'Nothing, not even the powers of hell, will stop my plans and purposes.'

The following week we received a fax from David and Jackie Townsend, who attend our church. On the day after the accident she wrote, 'In church on Sunday evening I saw a picture of a locomotive. It was huge. I have never seen such a powerful engine and it was just building up pressure and beginning to move. Nothing will stop it. If we stand in its way, it will smash us, but if we go with it, we will be caught up in the train.'

After Mary had written down what she had seen and

heard in the strange vision we took my mother and sister to visit the Esplanade, the beautiful gardens of Palmerston North. In the park is a native tree reserve, some outstanding rose gardens, numerous ponds with ducks and an aviary that is home to many famous New Zealand birds. As I looked at the birds I had no conception of how important an Australian cockatoo was shortly going to be to me. After passing by the cricket pitches next to the gardens, where scores of young boys sought to 'master willow and ball', we took my mother and sister back to Feilding.

With the afternoon to ourselves, we were eager to visit one of the local beaches. The nearest was Himatangi, a beach with firm sand that meant cars could be parked almost to the sea. On the way we stopped to browse around an antique furniture shop. The first settlers had brought much of the furniture from England and I thought of the stories each piece could have told had they been able to speak. The shop-keeper was eager to talk with us and when he discovered that we were going to the beach he suggested that we go to Waitarere instead. I thought about it, but decided to stay with the beach we had planned.

As we drove onto the sand of Himatangi Beach I was delighted to see that the surf was riding high and many people were racing up the beach on the breaking waves. There was a great sense of holiday and carnival, and as they played in the shallows children laughed and shouted to each other. Mary and I found a sheltered place near the sand dunes and she settled down to read. I ran across the sand and dived into the beckoning waves. For 40 minutes or more I body-surfed, enjoying terrific runs as the powerful waves rolled and broke onto the shore. I wondered if there was anything so exhilarating as hitching a free ride on such powerful carriers.

As I was swept forward on the breaking waves I became vaguely aware that the weather was changing and that above me grey clouds were building up. The sea was becoming more turbulent and without a wetsuit I began to feel cold. It was time to get out of the water and I walked out through the shallows towards where Mary was. Then suddenly, at the edge of the beach, I was struck by that irresistible urge that all true surfers know, to have 'just one more run'. I turned back towards the breaking surf.

Ignoring the cold, I swam out into the deep water where I could see the big waves building. There I waited, drifting in the lull for some time. After a number of false starts, I finally caught a beauty of a wave. I threw myself onto the rolling and surging water just as it was starting to break. Catching it perfectly, I felt the adrenalin flow through my body as I was thrust powerfully forward. The speed was incredible. I quickly gathered momentum as I raced towards the beach.

Suddenly, in a freak combination, two waves converged and broke under me. Without warning, I was catapulted out of the water and hurled crazily into the air. I crashed back down into the seething water. I found myself tossed about uncontrollably, as if I were in some giant washing machine.

I heard my neck bones crack. As my arms and hands lost feeling, pain surged across my back. I thought I was dying. 'Jesus, help me!' I cried aloud. Everything went black.

When consciousness returned I was lying like a piece of driftwood in the shallow water. Slowly I realized what had happened. The waves had washed me up. As I lay still I heard words being spoken audibly into my mind: 'When you pass through the waters, I will be with you; and when you pass through the rivers, they will not sweep over you. When you walk through the fire, you will not be burned.' In the weeks to come, I was to cling on for dear life to those prophetic words from Isaiah 43.

An intense pain pulsed through my neck and back. I struggled to my feet and made a few unsteady steps up the beach.

A large lady with tattoos going down to swim came towards me and I collapsed into her outstretched arms. As I lay on the wet sand, she cleared my mouth and dried my face and chest with a towel. Her compassion and kindness somehow seemed to reinforce the word the Lord had just spoken to me. As the woman sent her two children to bring Mary over, a young lifeguard with a shaven head arrived with blankets and he covered me.

Mary ran over to me. With her nursing training, she quickly realized that I had seriously damaged my neck. Forcing feelings of horror aside, she began to react professionally. Trying not to think about the implications, she decided that it was important that my head should be supported and made a neck brace for me with a towel. She was adamant that nobody should move me until professional medical help arrived. Much later, I realized that her persistence here may well have saved me from being completely paralysed.

I must have lain there on the sand for 30 minutes. With nothing to relieve the intensifying pain, it felt like an eternity. During that time I felt that the Lord was highlighting the words he had spoken to me earlier: 'When you walk through the fire, you will not be burned.' I reminded myself that although the fire was starting to heat up I would not be burned.

When the ambulance crew arrived, I pleaded with them for something for the pain. Reluctant to give me anything until they knew the extent of my injuries, they refused. Mary got into the ambulance with me and we set off to the hospital with the ambulance siren sounding.

On the way to the hospital the pain intensified again and I pleaded with them again. This time one of the officers radioed the hospital and as a result I was allowed some morphine. In fact it did little to alleviate the pain. As we drove on I recognized the crossroads where Mary and I had visited the antique shop. As we passed it, I thought of the time only a few hours earlier when we had looked together at the furniture and made that fateful decision to go to Himatangi.

After the 30-minute journey the Emergency Department at Palmerston North Hospital was a welcome sight. We stopped and I was wheeled into it on a trolley. I later learned that the lady with the tattoos followed the ambulance with our car and as Mary stepped out at the hospital she gave her the keys back and disappeared. We never even knew her name.

In the Emergency Department all I could think about was having something to relieve the agony as the registrar, Rob Rowan, examined me without comment. He called in a consultant, Mr McCormick, who arrived with his team and inspected me. His message for the scanning unit, which I was subsequently given, spelled out his fears. It said: 'Probably broken neck – please clarify.' The scanner did indeed clarify things, revealing the awful truth that I had broken four bones in my neck.

Now the medical team acted swiftly and I was taken to theatre. As I was being pushed towards it, Rob bent over and asked in a quiet, reassuring voice, 'Would you like me to pray over you?' Rob, a committed Christian, had no idea at that stage whether I even believed in God. I was just another patient he had to attend to.

In the theatre, two adjacent holes were bored into my skull. Two tongs were positioned into these and weights of 40 pounds were attached. The hope was that this weight would correct the dislocation of my neck and preserve the spinal cord intact until a further decision on treatment could be made. After the procedure, I was left in the theatre for a little time. Suddenly I felt the right-hand tong spring out of my skull. I grabbed it and held it in as I called for help. It was a moment of fire. Quickly Gordon, another registrar on the team, came to my aid and put the tong back.

Eventually I was taken out of the theatre to a private room. Here I was transferred from the ambulance trolley to a striker bed, an apparatus uneasily similar to a mortuary trolley. It was so narrow my shoulders completely filled the width. Joy, the staff nurse, made me comfortable, and just before I settled for the night she asked, 'Shall I pray over you before you sleep?'

After she left I lay there bewildered, thinking of all that had happened within the last seven hours. My mind went back to the celebration evening nearly three years earlier at Holy Trinity, Parr Mount, and the words that Irene the prophetess had spoken over me. They had been fulfilled exactly as she had said. I had indeed felt that I was drowning and dying. I had called to the Lord and he had indeed reached down his hand. And how true it was that 'he took hold of me, he drew me out of deep waters'.

Yet I needed all the comfort I could get. I was alive, but I felt I was still adrift in uncharted waters and being tossed around in a storm over which I had not the slightest control. My future was uncertain. My entire field of vision was reduced to one single square metre of ceiling. I could do nothing for myself. My every need – feeding, washing, pain control and even the use of bedpans – was now the responsibility of others. Terror and panic seemed to lurk around me.

Thankfully, Mary arrived and sat with me through that first awful night. As I repeatedly brought to mind the scriptures of hope given me on the beach, my terror was calmed. I believed I would survive. Finally, I fell into a fitful sleep only to be suddenly awakened and to be told mysteriously that it was time 'to be turned'. Two nurses appeared, placed a stretcher over my chest and legs, and then strapped me firmly into the striker bed. I was told to prepare myself to be rotated 180 degrees. At the count of three, they rotated me and I found myself staring at a floor that seemed to be spinning uncontrollably. I felt as if I were going to vomit. Then I was unstrapped and told by the nurses that they would return later and turn me the right side up. I began to feel like a barbecued chicken.

Over the next few days I came to dread the routine of 'being turned'. Six times a day this process was repeated and each time it happened I felt as if I were passing through the fire. Because of the vertigo and the feeling of sickness it always took time for me to settle down again afterwards.

My fear of that moment, when after every four hours I heard the sound of the approaching staff, was compounded when I heard the following conversation outside my room:

Nurse 1: 'The chap in there is on the striker bed and we are down to turn him.'

Nurse 2: 'Really! Have you much experience with those beds?'

Nurse 1: 'None! Although it was demonstrated at nursing school.'

Nurse 2: 'You know more about it than I do. I have never seen one.'

Nurse 1: 'Well, let's give it a try. I think you have to strap him in first.'

Nurse 2: 'You strap him in and I will turn him.'

By now sweat was flowing down my back as I had visions of being saved from the sea only to be dropped on the floor with my four broken neck bones by these well-meaning young women. Fortunately, a professional caution won through and a 'qualified striker turner' was summoned from sleep in the nurses' home.

In the weary week that followed, I began to get to know the hospital staff. There were regular visits from Rob Rowan and Mr McCormick. Gordon, the registrar who had helped put my tong back in the operating theatre, was also a frequent visitor to my bedside, usually accompanied by an entourage of nurses. Gordon loved his work and was renowned for operating at any time of the day or night. If he was on the orthopaedic unit, he often called in with Rob just to chat to me and Mary, claiming that it was 'always fun' talking with us. In turn, I came to call Rob and Gordon 'my boys'. The companionship and kindness I received from the staff were a boost to my morale in a difficult and painful week.

Every four hours, without fail, I went through the trauma of being turned. I was also regularly X-rayed, often twice a day, in order to check on the position of the dislocated bones and to try to determine the extent of the damage to my spinal cord. This process involved two orderlies pushing me on the striker bed along corridors and up lifts to the department. The trip always left me exhausted.

Back in my room, which I was now sure was going to be my home for many weeks, I stared up at the same small area of ceiling. I felt it was like lying on the deck of a boat, unable to see the sea but having a constant view of the sky. I found that it made me very disoriented and insecure.

At the end of the first week, Mr McCormick came in with other specialists to review the situation. It was not encouraging. The X-rays had shown that the weights had not been effective in righting the position of the broken bones. An operation was necessary. But where? One possibility was to fly me by helicopter to a specialist neurological unit in either Auckland or Christchurch, and my condition was discussed with the consultants there. Mary and I considered things and requested that I be moved to Auckland. All that was needed was for Mr McCormick to make the final decision. Mary started to pack up and plan her drive to Auckland.

On the Friday afternoon, Mr McCormick visited me alone. He admitted to being very perplexed about the whole situation and not quite sure what further action to take. Clearly the weights were not going to produce the desired effect. However, he had also come to the conclusion that my neck was too unstable for me to be moved. Indeed, he felt that the condition of my neck was so delicate that I could not even be moved from the narrow striker bed. Whatever happened next would have to be at Palmerston North Hospital and on this bed.

Faced with the dilemma of how to treat me, Mr McCormick decided to consider matters carefully. He had a boat on Marlborough Sound and said that as he was fishing over the weekend he would review my condition. On Monday he would make a decision. I told him that I would ask Jesus to give him wisdom. His reply was that he would not use that terminology, but he would be meditating.

For me the weekend seemed endless. The seriousness of the situation had finally begun to make its full impact upon me. For the last week I had been carried along with all the activity that had constantly surrounded me and had not had time to stop and face the implications of my accident. Now I was forced to face them. What I knew did not encourage me. I was all too aware that Christopher Reeve, who had played 'Superman', had broken just one neck bone and now, confined to a wheelchair, was paralysed from the neck down and able to breathe only with the assistance of a machine. And I had four broken bones in my neck.

For the first time I acknowledged to myself the extent of my injuries. My arms told me the seriousness of my case: apart from the upper parts and my thumbs and index fingers, they were quite numb. Was I going to be a cripple? Would I ever walk again? Mr McCormick's hesitation had not helped my mood. I knew from the hospital staff that he was a brilliant surgeon with decades of experience, so if he felt my case was not straightforward then there had to be the real possibility that everything could go very badly wrong. In my worry, again and again I kept repeating the promise of the Lord to me: 'When you walk through the fire, you will not be burned.'

It was late on Monday afternoon when Mr McCormick came to my room and sat down by my bed. For some time we talked about fishing and boats. Then he looked straight at me. 'Barry,' he said simply, 'I've booked a theatre and will operate on you in the morning.'

He asked whether I would like to know the full details and implications of the operation, or whether I would just submit myself to the process. I told him that I wanted to know everything he could tell me. In quiet, assured tones he outlined the difficulties as he saw them. My condition was anything but straightforward. Because of the nature of the multiple breaks, the whole neck region was very unstable and nerves could easily be broken or damaged. The X-rays had not been very revealing because the angles were difficult and they had only shown a very limited amount of information. Only when he had opened me up would he be able to see the full extent of my injuries. There could be further problems if there were crumpled or broken bones in the front of my neck.

With regard to the practicalities of the operation, Mr McCormick told me that he intended to make an incision of about ten inches that would stretch from the top to the bottom of my neck. Another six-inch incision would be made in my pelvis from which bone would be taken and grafted onto my broken neck bones in order to try and repair them. Then, gently, he came to the worst-case scenario. If the operation didn't work I would wake up paralysed from my neck down. As I tried to control my shock at the prospect of being a quadriplegic, he told me that he fully intended to give the operation his best shot and that he was optimistic about the results.

As he left, Murray, the Australian anaesthetist, came in, bending a black tube in his hands. He began by commiserating with me about what I had just been told and then proceeded to give me further bad news. Because of the risks involved, he would not be able to give me a pre-med anaesthetic until he had carried out a number of preliminary actions. Furthermore, because I would have to have my operation on the striker bed, a number of major procedures would have to be completed before I could be turned and anaesthetized. Shaken, I listened as he told me in detail what he would be doing when we met in the operating theatre. He would start by putting two tubes down my nostrils and squirting in a substance. As I felt it going in, I was to inhale deeply. Then he would cut a little hole in my throat and feed in another tube, down which a further substance would be pumped. Once I felt these substances entering my body I was to indicate this to him by raising my thumb. By then, he would have put a needle in my arm and at my signal would inject me with anaesthetic.

As Murray left I realized that neither man had given the impression that this was going to be in any sense a straightforward operation. Yet despite being badly shaken by what I had heard, I continued to have a deep peace inside me. I knew that friends in England were praying for me and I felt sustained by their prayers, despite the uncertainty of my situation. I turned to Mary, who had by now become a part of my nursing team, and told her that I would very much appreciate it if someone could come and anoint me with oil and pray over me. I had barely spoken these words when an unexpected visitor arrived. Introducing himself as Nigel, a pastor from the local community church, he said that he had heard about us and had felt compelled to come and visit us that evening. He asked if I would like him to anoint me with oil and pray. Before he did this, however, Nigel said that he had a scripture that had come to him as he travelled to the hospital. Reaching for Mary's Bible he read: 'When you pass through the waters, I will be with you; and when you pass through the rivers, they will not sweep over you. When you walk through the fire, you will not be burned; the flames will not set you ablaze.' The words were exactly those that the Lord had spoken into my heart as I lay on the beach immediately after the accident.

I awoke early on the morning of the operation with the sombre thought that this day I really would be 'riding the storm'. Mary came to be with me before I went to the theatre. She was a constant source of love and hope and never expressed the agony that I knew she must have been suffering.

As the orderlies came for me at seven I told myself again that the Lord had promised that when I walked through fire I would not be burned. So far I felt that I had passed through many minor fires, but I knew that this was going to be the really big one. 'Jesus, help me,' I said aloud, and as I entered the theatre a great peace seemed to embrace and enfold me.

In the theatre I was met by all three orthopaedic surgeons: Mr McCormick, Rob and Gordon. I could see Murray the anaesthetist stretching his tubes and the team of nurses preparing the instruments. We were ready.

The operation started. Quickly and efficiently, Murray performed the procedures he had described to me. Two tubes disappeared up my nose and I felt cold liquid entering. A scalpel cut a slit in my throat and another tube was inserted. Suddenly my chest and upper body were filled with some strange substance. As I raised my thumb to indicate the substances were taking effect, Murray quickly pushed the plunger of the syringe attached to the needle in my arm. For a strange moment I felt as if I were falling backwards and cried yet again, 'Jesus, help me!'

Unconsciousness slipped over me.

3
The Dark Valley

As I was taken into the operating theatre Mary, who had been allowed to stay in the 'on-call' residences within the hospital, went to pray in the hospital chapel. Mr McCormick had anticipated that the operation would probably take between three and four hours and had started at 8 a.m. At noon Mary telephoned the ward to be told that the operation was still in progress and that, as yet, there was no news. Having had a career in nursing, she became apprehensive and began wondering whether the team had met a bigger problem than expected. Unable to concentrate, she went back to where she was staying, took all her clothes out of their drawers and ironed them. Then, to try and distract her mind, she sat down and wrote out all the different words she could make up out of the words 'NO SMOKING' that were on the sign above the door.

At 1 p.m. she telephoned the ward again, only to be told that there was still no news from theatre. Increasingly concerned, she called the ward again shortly afterwards and asked them to phone theatre to find out what was happening. Finally, at 2 p.m., theatre phoned her to say that the operation had gone well and she could go down to the recovery room. I had been in the surgeons' hands for over six hours.

It turned out that when Mr McCormick had opened me up he had discovered a piece of bone had broken off the underside of my neck. He had to wire this back on and then wire the other damaged vertebrae together. Then finally the grafted bone from the pelvis was used to rebuild the broken bones. When I saw the X-ray pictures later I felt his achievement looked like a work of art. Later still, I found out by experience that the amount of wire used was enough to set off airport security alarms.

I slowly regained consciousness at about 3 p.m. My first thought on waking was to discover whether I was paralysed. With fear and trepidation, I slowly and cautiously moved my hands down my body. Except for half of my hands and arms, which were still without feeling, I had sensation elsewhere. I was normal! I started to weep with relief.

Back in my room the euphoria waned. The weights were reapplied and the four-hourly turns on the striker were renewed. A new nightmare began, and this time the pain in my neck, back and shoulders was immense. I was given a syringe device that released doses of morphine at the press of a button when the pain became unbearable. Pain alleviation came almost immediately, but I found the ability to hover in a cocoon of tranquillity above the pain almost addictive. Because any form of clothing took so long to change and as all my movements were painful, I had to be nursed naked. Unable to move my neck or head I returned to my view of the patch of ceiling above me.

Naked, unable to move, in pain and forced to stare at a fixed spot, I found myself more vulnerable than I had ever been in my life. Although the operation was over, the medical team would give no guarantee of my future. On at least two occasions I had given myself into the hands of God, not knowing whether I would die or be paralysed for life. I had to do so again.

Now, lying there on the striker bed, I found myself slowly beginning a deep reappraisal of much of my Christian faith. Nearly 40 years earlier I had come to know and trust Jesus and had been befriended by evangelical Christians who had led me to discover the Bible's rich and wonderful revelation of the living God. I had been ordained into the Anglican Church and, apart from a few years, had spent my entire ministry on the staff of St Andrew's, Chorleywood. However, neither my background nor my tradition seemed to equip me for the situation I found myself in now. My experience of God had been through worship, prayer and reading the Scriptures. Now I sometimes found that I could not even put my prayers into words. With so much of what I had relied on before taken away from me, it was all I could do simply to seek God's presence.

In this dark valley of pain, fear and uncertainty, my relationship with Jesus seemed to be confined to basic utterances such as 'Lord, help me!', 'It hurts!', 'I'm frightened!', 'I feel panicky!', 'I don't want to die.' My hope focused around no more than simply letting go of everything and resting in his invisible arms. I gave thanks for the apparently small things that were done for me. After a bed bath or a pain-relieving injection, I would affirm the nurses and say, 'Thank you, Lord.' In a different way, I understood that God was always with me. I would often say to God, 'I know you are there,' and I was reminded of the words of David the psalmist, 'The Lord is ever before me, he is at my right hand.'

Reading the word of God has always been very important to me, but now I was unable to hold a book. Initially, Mary read short passages of Scripture aloud to me. Eventually, I devised a plan that turned out to be a daily source of hope and comfort. Mid-morning was usually wash time, after which the striker bed was turned so that I faced downwards. Now, instead of staring at the ceiling, I could see the floor through a round hole in the frame of the bed. When I was in this position, a nurse would place an open Bible underneath the bed. The staff all knew I was reading the prophet Isaiah, so part of their routine became to turn the pages to the appropriate chapter for the day. In my vulnerability and pain, this word revealed to me a world of hope that lay outside the confines of a striker bed.

A far more down-to-earth matter involved cricket. I have always been a cricket fan and England were touring New Zealand at that time. One of the orderlies who regularly and carefully took me to the X-ray department arranged an ingenious system of mirrors around and above my bed so that I was able to watch the games on television.

In the hope that I would indeed be able to walk again I started a routine of stretching exercises. As I lay immobile on my back I would raise my legs six inches off the bed and hold them there to the count of ten. Each day I did a series of these and followed them by pulling my legs towards me and stretching them as far as they would go. At times, the exertion was so much that I found myself sweating.

Another strain centred on a change in the way I was given painkillers. The button-controlled injector was taken away, with the promise that I could now have morphine from the nurses on request. This meant that I was now entirely dependent upon the nurses hearing my demands for painkillers. During the day this was not a problem, but during the night, when there might be only two nurses on the ward and both very busy, it was a different matter. At lights-out I was given a switch that would ring a bell in the nurses' bay, and before going to sleep I would try and secure this firmly around my wrist. Sometimes, however, the bell switch slipped off onto the floor. Then, if I woke in the early hours of the morning, as I often did, with an intense pain in my neck and back, it was sometimes difficult to get the attention of a nurse. As the pain increased, I would begin to panic, calling, 'Nurse! Nurse!' Often the nurses would be busy at the other end of the ward and unable to hear me in my cubicle. Finally, just when I thought I couldn't bear the pain any longer, a nurse would appear on a routine check of the ward. Even then it seemed to take for ever before I received my morphine. The nurse had to get keys and take the drug from a locked cabinet, then she had to make entries in a logbook. Finally she had to find someone to sign an authorization for its use. Losing the bell became something I dreaded.

One day a team of six nurses arrived with the announcement that they were going to transfer me to a new bed. This electrically controlled bed had a press-button attachment that raised the upper part of the mattress a few degrees and it was faced towards the window. For the first time since entering the hospital I had a view of the outside world!

With the new bed, something that had been an unremarkable everyday matter took on a profound, inspirational meaning. With my head set in its fixed position I found I was able to see through the top of my bedroom window. I looked westward. I couldn't see the city of Palmerston North (that would have been visible through the bottom half of the window). Instead, my view was of the line of hills beyond that stretched right across my rigid, unchanging field of vision.

In the mornings, I was often awoken by the soft fresh early light as it started to climb slowly up the hills. I must have seen hundreds of sunrises before but I had never in my life been so appreciative of the sheer beauty of the approaching day. As I watched, the light would inch up the valleys like water rising in a canal lock; dark shadows gave way to the light yellow glow of the summer grass, and trees and shrubs appeared as if they had been placed there by an invisible hand. Above the hills, the sky slowly lit up with a wonderful translucent glow. Each morning, I felt as if I were witnessing the creation of the world. Around me the hospital would still be in silence and I could imagine that I was the only person on the planet. The phrase 'in the beginning God created' echoed in my mind and filled me with awe and wonder. In the darkness of the night, after being awakened to be turned or injected, I would lie still, longing to see God at work again in the sunrise.

In the evenings, it was different. If it had been a sunny day, by late afternoon I was as expectant as if I were some concert-goer who had just taken his seat at the Royal Festival Hall to hear Beethoven's 'Pastoral Symphony'. Only instead of sitting in a concert hall waiting for the music to begin, I lay instead immobile in my bed, eagerly awaiting the grandeur to begin. As I watched, the fiery ball of the sun sank gently down over the hills and edged slowly out of sight. The lower it sank, the greater the intensity of the colours became until finally, in a flashing crescendo of dazzling colour, it disappeared and the sky above exploded in a breathtaking display as the dying rays struck the wispy hovering clouds. As I watched this show of splendour I was always reminded that the heavens were 'the work of his hands'. And when the sun had finally set I would meditate on all I had seen and experienced and utter praises and thanksgivings. It was just as well that the dawn and sunset were such blessings because very soon the effects of trauma began to break through into my mind and emotions.

I started having flashbacks. My first flashback came, I think, either in a dream or just as I awoke from sleep. Suddenly I was landing in the wave and could feel the sheer fear and panic as my body spun round uncontrollably. It was as if all my nightmares had been condensed into one single, overwhelming experience. I felt as if I were trapped in a cage underwater and couldn't breathe. I was spinning like a Catherine wheel. I had lost all control over my situation and I knew I was drowning. I experienced again the exact moment that my neck was broken, hearing the terrible cracking sound and flinching as the searing pain flashed through my body. I was dying. There was no one to help me. I tensed my muscles and held my breath. I was aware that my body was bathed in sweat and that my head was wet. This was the end of my life. I started to shake and sob uncontrollably.

The flashbacks came like sudden storms. Without warning, their fury would strike and overwhelm me. When finally they blew themselves out, I was left weak, shaken and disoriented. I soon realized that at some stage I would have to 'face the unfaceable'. Somehow I had to come to terms with my terrible accident and my brush with death.

Coping with the flashbacks was not easy. The problem was that when they struck, I immediately and instinctively went into a mental survival mode in which I was unable to handle the sensations that overwhelmed me. Although I found these experiences terrifying, I found myself reluctantly admitting that from a pastoral point of view they were illuminating. In the past people had often confided in me regarding traumas they had had which had affected them for months. In ignorance, I had often felt like simply telling them to pull themselves together. Now though, in a similar situation, I realized that finding a solution was outside my control.

I decided to try and pre-empt the flashbacks by running through the accident in my own mind. Lying on my bed, I gently and cautiously tried to force myself to re-enact the events. In my mind's eye I could see myself swimming out to where the big waves were forming. There I would float in the lull as the new waves started to swell and grow about me. Finally, I would catch the big one. But as I did, an almost physical sensation of panic and fear gripped me and I immediately had to cast the moment from my mind. I realized that I was unable to cope even with reliving events in my mind. I needed help.

Thinking about the problem, I reminded myself that Jesus had come to 'bind up the broken-hearted and set the captives free'. How I needed both of these ministries! But how could Jesus help me? The answer came to me when I recalled that, at the moment of greatest danger, I had cried out, 'Jesus, help me!' That I was still alive was a witness to the fact that he *had* helped me. Somehow he had intervened in the tumult of the wave. As it occurred to me that at the very moment of my terror Jesus had in fact been there, I realized what I had to do. I had to see him there when I came to relive the accident. Because the flashback was too overwhelming, I decided to try and rerun the situation in my imagination. As I tried again, I saw myself being thrown up into the air by the waves and landing in the swirling surf. Suddenly Jesus was there. I felt like one of the disciples caught in a storm on the Sea of Galilee. He had seen Jesus coming towards him walking on the water, had called for help and Jesus had intervened. The storm had been stilled and peace had followed. So, in my own turmoil, I knew Jesus was with me. Amid the panic and the pain, I felt his presence. From that time onwards the sting of the flashbacks was taken away. They didn't cease immediately, but I now experienced them without the feeling of terror. The effects of trauma were in fact to continue for months, but I will return to them later.

Many people commented on what they felt was the extraordinary way I had faced the surgery and its attending procedures. In fact this was simply the grace of God, as I felt that the traumas had been dealt with through God's presence with me. Often the words of Mr McCormick and Murray the anaesthetist would come to me and I would relive how I had been prepared for the operation. Again and again, as I tried to face the past, I sought to see Jesus in every last detail of what had happened.

In addition to having the comfort of the Holy Spirit that gave a deep peace in my heart, I soon discovered that I had an innate need and desire for human comfort. For over ten years I had travelled extensively in New Zealand, leading teams on national tours and speaking at conferences and celebrations.

In fact returning from one trip, I told Mary that I had now spoken in every major city; unimpressed she simply told me it was the privilege of ministry. The result of these contacts was that many people kindly and sacrificially visited us.

As the visitors came I tried to find meaning and learn lessons from everything that happened around my bed. I had always found that one of the incredible privileges of being in the ordained ministry was visiting the sick and dying, and I had sat or stood at many bedsides. I had, however, never experienced ill health myself or understood how vulnerable one could be. There were further lessons to learn.

Let me put the visits in context. I was lying on my back, stretched by a weight from my head, and quite unable to move. Indeed, it was only with difficulty that I could see the visitors at all, fixed as I was facing up at the ceiling. I soon realized that the visitors standing at the end of the bed were of varying categories.

Many well-meaning people came on what they obviously saw as a divine mission. Some arrived rather noisily and full of faith. They came with a variety of helps. First, they had books on how Jesus heals today, supplemented by more books on the ways in which God had miraculously healed individuals. Standing at the end of my bed, they would give me a résumé of each book. Usually this ministry to the captive audience was accompanied by a gift of a box full of audio tapes by famous Christians who had been dramatically used by God to heal the sick. And again their story was usually told in full. By the end of their visit, I was utterly exhausted, frustrated and screaming inside. It often took me hours to regain my peace.

Other visitors would spend the time patiently telling me about themselves and the ministry God was giving them. They would take me at length on their ministry tours to meet the famous people whom they knew personally. Then they would discuss with me their latest book and the way in which God had used them in large conferences. This was also exhausting.

Yet another group were the friends of friends' friends. Often they had heard from some telephone call from England that I was in hospital and had come for an afternoon's outing. Often we had little common ground because they were so far removed from anyone I knew personally that they ended up sitting adjacent to me in complete silence for what seemed like for ever. At such times, I would feel obliged to initiate conversation, something that drained me. Thankfully Mary saw what was happening and soon started to filter people at the door.

One visit we were really looking forward to was that of John and Heather Cowen from Chorleywood. For days we anticipated the joy of seeing familiar faces from England. They gave great encouragement as they brought us up to date with home news.

I began to appreciate that there was such a thing as emotional energy. Like physical energy it could, under certain circumstances, drain away very quickly. Following the operation my resources of emotional energy had clearly been heavily reduced and I needed to be alone to rest and recharge after a visit.

In those early days in the hospital, the visits I appreciated most of all were those of the friends who would speak little but just quietly sit there holding my hand for five minutes or so, and then say a short prayer before leaving. I found this type of visit a great comfort. Afterwards, I was able in silence to gain strength as I remembered what they had said both in their words and silences.

One night I had a strange and vivid experience. It was a recollection of the events on Himatangi Beach, but I was certain that it was not a flashback, as I had none of the fear that was associated with them. Starting when I called out,

'Jesus, help me!' it was followed by what seemed to be almost a video of scenes and people. I could see myself struggling up the beach and falling into the arms of the large tattooed lady. Next, I was lying on the beach with the skin-head lifeguard running up with blankets. I seemed to sense how very concerned and caring he was. Now little children appeared, bringing Mary over to where I lay. As I watched, the professionals arrived and I saw the ambulance officers take control. Now the images seemed to jump and I could see myself in my room on the ward. I watched a particular nurse tend me and I was aware of her kindness and sympathy. There was another jump and I saw the orderly arranging the mirrors for me to watch the cricket. When the sequence of images finished there seemed to be a silence in my mind. I lay there thinking about all that I had seen. As I did, I seemed to hear the Lord speak: 'You asked me to help you and I did, but which of these people would you have chosen?'

Tears rolled down my cheeks. My answer, I knew, was probably none of them. I realized how selective I had been in so many aspects of my life and relationships. I felt grieved as it came to me how I had either ignored or undervalued so many people. I was reminded again that this is God's world and that he can use people from all walks of life as his servants.

It was a lesson I knew I should have learned much earlier in life. In fact, I had had a remarkable demonstration of the same principle years earlier when I first arrived in England at the end of my 12,000-mile journey from New Zealand. Travel-weary and virtually penniless, I had arrived with my backpack at Dover dressed in shorts and tee shirt and, unsurprisingly, had been given a thorough search by a customs officer. It was late in the afternoon by the time I left the port and I realized that with the sum total of my wealth being five pounds it was going to be difficult to make my way to the only contacts I had in England, a family in Hampshire. 'Jesus, help me!' I said as I walked up the road. Suddenly the customs officer who had searched me stopped in his car and offered me a lift. When I said I was making my way to Hampshire, he told me that it was too late in the day to try and invited me to spend the night at his home. When we arrived at his council house, he had opened the back door and called out to his wife, telling her that they had a guest for the night. To my astonishment, she had replied that she knew someone would be coming. Early that day she had had so strong a conviction that they were going to have a visitor that evening that she had not only cooked an extra meal but had set a third place at the table! As God had used the customs officer, so now he had used nurses, tattooed ladies and skinhead lifeguards.

It was one more lesson learned. There were to be many others.

4
Reflections From Immobility

In all, I was horizontal, barely able to move and restricted as to what I could see for seven weeks. During that time, I was able to think over all sorts of things. Something that I thought about a lot was how God spoke to me.

While lying on my back, confined to one place for such a long period, I found that I had a problem knowing what was real and what was not. My prayers took the form of a general chat to God. This was intermittent during the day and more frequent during the many long and lonely nights. As part of this, I would often hear a voice in my mind. My dilemma was discerning when this was indeed the voice of God or when it was an illusion, generated in my imagination by my own wishes and desires. The problem was made worse by the fact that at this time I really wanted to hear what God had to say to me. The result was that I was forced to think through everything that I had come to believe about how God spoke to me through his written word and directly through his voice. There, on my hospital bed, as I struggled with this I went over in my mind some of the situations I had been involved in where God had spoken directly to myself and others.

The Christian tradition in which I had been schooled had

taught me that while God communicated something of his nature through creation, he spoke mainly through the Scriptures. That this was the whole story was something that became challenged when I joined the staff of St Andrew's, Chorleywood, in September 1971. On the Monday morning members of the church welcomed me over coffee and cakes in the church hall. There the warden Iain Roberts gave me a scripture from Deuteronomy 31, which he had written out. This recorded the words of Moses to Joshua as he was handing over command: 'Be strong and courageous, for you must go with this people into the land that the LORD swore to their forefathers to give them, and you must divide it among them as their inheritance. The LORD himself goes before you and will be with you; he will never leave you nor forsake you. Do not be afraid; do not be discouraged' (vv. 7–8).

These words were to be prophetic for me, outlining what I have been seeking to do during the last 27 years. They apply especially to the Faith Sharing Teams, where my aim has been to encourage individuals and congregations into experiencing the various waves of the Holy Spirit that have flowed through the churches. During this work, I have always looked to the Scriptures to lead and guide me. At particular times, I would find that God would often underline certain truths and I would act in response to them.

One morning, early in my ministry at Chorleywood, I had an experience in which God spoke to me in a very different way. Mary had taken our young children to school and I had gone into my study to pray. As I opened the door, I heard a voice. It was that of a man speaking in normal tones and it said simply, 'I will direct you.' I was taken completely by surprise. The voice had been so normal and so audible that I looked around the room for the speaker. There was no one there and I ran up the stairs to search in the bedrooms for the man who had spoken to me. Again, there was no one.

Bemused, I returned to the study where I sat down quietly. Gradually it dawned on me that what I had heard was the Lord speaking a direct word of promise to me.

I found this experience both exciting and challenging. It extended my expectation of the ways in which God might communicate with me. I realized that both the Scriptures and this direct spoken word of God were prophetic. This concept of prophecy came to grip me as I saw the impact both types of promise had made on my life.

Since then, I have come to believe that God speaks in different ways. The first way is where someone hears an apparently human voice speaking words in their own language from somewhere around them. This in my experience is rare, and the case I have just recounted is the only one that has ever happened to me. The second type is a more internal voice that sounds, as it were, 'in the heart', although this can be so real that it feels as if someone is speaking to you.

My first experience of this second type in fact predated my time at Chorleywood and occurred when I was serving as a curate at Camborne Parish Church in Cornwall. There Michael, a young man I knew slightly, was involved in a head-on collision. His car was destroyed and he was rushed off to Treliske Hospital. When I heard of the accident some days later, I immediately went to see him. He was in the intensive care unit and there I spoke with the team who had responsibility for him. His prognosis was hopeless and the consultant thought that he only had a day or two to live. With that sombre verdict in my mind, I went into his cubicle to see him. Michael lay there, numerous tubes coming out from him into a variety of machines and a nurse by his head solemnly monitoring the situation. We nodded to each other, maintaining the silence. As I was about to pray over him I heard an audible inner voice say, 'He will live.'

Confused, I stared at the bandaged figure before me, his bloodied nose protruding from the dressings, an oxygen mask helping him as he gasped for breath. What I had heard was contrary to the expert medical opinion I had been given, and what I saw gave me no grounds to question that verdict. Yet, without doubt, I knew I had heard a voice say, 'He will live.' Feeling perplexed, I told the nurse that I was going to offer a prayer for Michael. As I started to pray, I found myself hoping that she would not hear what I was about to say. Then I gently laid my hands on his head and prayed, 'Lord Jesus, I thank you that you are going to heal Michael. I ask right now that you will flood his body with your healing power.' That very day restoration started. When I next visited Michael later in the week he was sitting up without tubes, and the bandages had been removed from his scarred face.

In my ministry at Chorleywood I came to see that this type of direct and clearly audible inner voice from God often said something contrary to what I naturally saw and expected. Often it was in the context of sickness and was associated with the person being physically healed. At other times, I have found God speaking to me in a less dramatic way – in a way so ordinary in fact that it is hardly discernible from one's own thoughts, but, like the promises of Scripture, these words are usually 'underlined' in the heart. This process has been described as 'inner knowing' and is, in its very nature, hard to rationalize.

Jesus himself was to say in the context of a spectacular healing that 'the Son can do nothing by himself; he can only do what he sees his Father doing' (John 5:19). The circumstances under which he said these words are very enlightening. In Jerusalem then there was a pool called Bethesda where many disabled people would gather seeking healing. It seems that from time to time the waters of the pool were mysteriously disturbed and the belief was that the first one into the pool at this time would be healed. When Jesus visited the pool, he walked down through the crowds of sick people and stopped in front of a man who had been an invalid for 38 years. He asked him whether he wanted to be healed. The man, who had no idea who Jesus was, replied that there was no one available to put him in the pool when the waters were disturbed. Plainly his hope for healing was in being lowered into the pool, not in the person of Jesus. Yet Jesus was able to order the man, 'Get up! Pick up your mat and walk.' To have such confidence, under such unpromising conditions, Jesus must have heard the Father's inner audible voice being spoken to him.

Sometimes I have found that this distinct inner voice focused not on physical healing but on the setting free of a person from events in the past that still had a destructive hold on their life. One illustration of this occurred when my colleague James Roberts and I were ministering at a conference for young leaders in Finland near a beautiful lake at the centre of the country. At one coffee break, as I walked past the queue, I saw a young woman who immediately caught my attention. Had I met her before, I wondered, and if so where? I stopped and looked at her at least three times and just as I was about to move on I heard the inner audible voice say, 'She ran away from home.' I was surprised as I could not see how, in any way, it could be relevant. Later that afternoon I took my interpreter and sought the girl out. After talking together about the conference, I was just about to ask her whether she had in fact run away from home when the inner audible voice suddenly said, 'When she was 14.' Taking my courage in both hands I asked her, 'When you were 14 did you run away from home?' She stared at me in absolute incredulity. It was true, she admitted, but how did I know? I simply said that Jesus had told me. I didn't know what else to say and suggested that, if she wished, we could talk again at some later time.

On the last day of the conference, the girl met with me and shared the impact that God's prophetic word had made on her. She had been brought up in a Christian family and always believed that Jesus was present, knew everything and answered prayers. The only problem she had was that what she believed always applied to other people and not to her. Jesus always seemed to be a personal friend of others, not her. However, what I had said to her had shaken her. She said to me, 'If Jesus told a person I never knew, who did not speak my language, something that only I and my family knew, then he must know everything about me.' Realization of this truth, which is reflected in Psalm 139, had begun a transformation in her life.

I also discovered in my ministry that this inner audible voice could confront a person with the truth about themselves and God. One of the best illustrations I know of this comes, not from my own life, but from my daughter Noonie. One warm summer's evening she had been out with friends and was returning to her flat in Hammersmith. She suggested to her friends that they get off the bus two stops before their normal stop and walk home together. As they walked and chatted she suddenly became conscious of a middle-aged man walking along with a young boy ahead of them. Noonie felt what she could only describe as 'an inner stirring of the Holy Spirit'. Suddenly she left her friends and started to run up the road towards the man and the boy. As she reached them, she heard the audible inner voice of Jesus speaking to her. She stopped the well-dressed businessman. 'You are a member of a homosexual ring,' she told him, 'and you are seducing this boy for homosexual purposes and you have offered him money.' At this, the man became furious and started to curse and swear. Noonie turned to the youth and asked him whether the man had in fact offered him money to be involved in homosexual activity. The boy replied that he had. 'Do you want to go with him or us?' Noonie asked. Perplexed and frightened the boy replied, 'With you.' Now the man started to become physically violent. Noonie and her friends grabbed hold of the boy and ran away down the street with him. Later on in the flat over a meal they explained to the boy, who appeared very naïve, the danger he had exposed himself to. During the early hours of the morning they were able to tell him, in response to his questions, about Jesus and his love for him. Before the boy went to sleep on the sofa he asked that they would pray for him that he too might know Jesus.

This same inner audible voice of God that confronts a person with the truth can also bring incredible hope to the hopeless. Our son Timothy lives in Harrow on the Hill. On one occasion, he and his brother Jonathan were having a drink together at the local pub. As they did, a man in his early 30s came in and sat down by himself at a nearby table. He kept watching them and then suddenly stood up and walked over to their table. Looking at Jonathan he said, 'I see that you are a man of integrity.'

Jonathan found himself taken completely by surprise. 'Have you anything to say to me?' the stranger continued.

Jonathan found himself saying, 'Jesus loves you.'

The young man started to weep. Jonathan suddenly heard the inner audible voice speak to him. Repeating what he had heard he said simply, 'I see you are dying.'

'Yes,' came the quiet reply. 'I am dying of AIDS.'

My sons invited the stranger to join them. He was obviously looking for someone to listen to him and soon told them something of what had happened to him. Being diagnosed with AIDS had sent him into a panic. Distraught, he had boarded a train that morning and got off at Harrow. He had spent most of the day walking around the town asking God continuous questions. 'If you are God how can I possibly know you?' 'What will happen to me when I die?' 'Is there some way that you can communicate with me?' Finally, completely worn out and exhausted, he had walked into the pub. Sitting down he had scanned those present and his eyes had fallen upon Jonathan. As he watched him, he had had a growing impression that somehow he had the answer to his questions. Together, Jonathan and Timothy tried as best they could to answer his questions, and at the end of the evening the man had come to realize that the answer to his questions lay with Jesus Christ. They told him of how, in his death and resurrection, Jesus had dealt with the problem of people's separation from God and how in Jesus a believer could receive forgiveness and eternal life. As the evening ended, the man asked for prayer and together the brothers prayed for him. There, around the pub table, the man received hope.

I had also come to see in my ministry that God reveals himself not just through giving words but also in giving visions. Sometimes a vision can seem so real that the person to whom it occurs can feel that they are in the situation physically. There was once a Norwegian pastor on a course that we conducted for clergy. As I prayed over him one evening, I saw three icy mountain peaks that were being melted by the sun. In the context of his ministry and church, I thought that they represented situations that God was about to melt. I was surprised when he abruptly left the room. It turned out that he had felt angry with me because he thought that I was implying that he had a cold heart. The next day he went to London and visited Westminster Cathedral. There, sitting in a chapel, he looked up to see a three-dimensional image of Jesus suspended on the cross above him. Transfixed, he stared at the realistic image and suddenly overwhelmed he realized that he did indeed have a cold heart. He started to cry. When he told me of his experience and asked my forgiveness, he cried again.

Mary's experience on the morning of my accident was something like this. In such cases, the images almost seem to imprint themselves on the mind and can be watched again and again rather like a film. As I was lying on the hospital bed two experiences of such visions came to mind.

The first was when Mary and I had been invited to lead a weekend houseparty for St Paul's, Onslow Square, a church plant from Holy Trinity Brompton. During a time of worship, I vividly saw two doors and I knew that they symbolized the doors to heaven. Suddenly and unexpectedly, I saw an angel come out and stand before the half-open door. As I watched I heard him say, 'The Lord is anointing the prophets.'

I was due to speak after the worship. During my talk, I tried to bring some contemporary truth from the prophecies of Joel and duly finished at the allotted time. My final words started like this, 'We are now breaking for coffee. This will be served at a number of locations around the auditorium. Do feel free to go now.' However, instead of ending here I felt compelled to say, 'However, the Lord is anointing the prophets.' As I said these words, about 15 of the 400 or so people present fell immediately onto the floor. Many others stood shaking from head to foot under the inspiration of the Holy Spirit. Realizing what was happening I said, 'If you have been affected by this word, please come to the front while the others go for coffee.' As those who were not already on the floor assembled at the front, many more people began to fall down under the Spirit's power. The Spirit had indeed anointed the prophets.

The second, and perhaps my most vivid, experience of such a direct and distinct vision was at a New Wine conference. I had been invited to speak at the last evening of the conference and I had set the day aside to pray and fast as I prepared for the evening meeting. During the afternoon, I had gone up onto the hills above the farm where we regularly stayed. Over the eight years I had helped at the conference, these hills had become a special place for me and I had acquired the habit of taking a prayer walk with our dog,

Sophie, every morning just before six o'clock. In the quietness there we often saw rabbits, foxes, deer, birds and even the occasional badger. That afternoon I sat down to pray on the peak of the hill overlooking the farm, with the town of Glastonbury behind me. Suddenly, as I sat there, I seemed to vividly see an enormously wide and bulky carpet stretching out before me. As I watched, I felt sure that it had something to do with the ministry of the Holy Spirit.

I have often found that actually speaking at very large gatherings can be something of an anticlimax. The thoughtful and prayerful preparation for a talk can take a very long time and all the tensions and concerns of speaking before thousands build up within you. Then, suddenly and abruptly, it is all over. In addition, I have often found that there is an enormous conflict within me over what I feel I have been given to say and what I feel I am expected to say. This night was no different. At the end of my talk, I asked the gathering in the auditorium to stand. As they rose to their feet in the downstairs area and in the horseshoe-shaped balcony, I found the sight of so many people standing together awesome. Then I invited the Holy Spirit to come and do among us what Jesus had sent him to do.

The silence was heavy and pregnant. As we waited, I suddenly saw the carpet again, but this time it straddled the back of the auditorium and seemed to stretch above the balcony. I knew that those sitting there had to welcome the Holy Spirit. I felt strangely aware that what was to happen that evening depended on their response. I encouraged those in the balcony to open their hearts and say, 'Come, Holy Spirit.' As I said this, the Spirit fell in power upon those in the far part of the balcony. From the stage where I was, this looked strange. Hundreds of people in the balcony were being affected by the presence of the Spirit, while the majority below were completely unmoved. Then I had the thought that for God to move from the balcony area everyone had to welcome the Holy Spirit. I felt a sense of great urgency. It seemed to me that God's will to bless the people hinged on their consciously calling upon him. I made this known and it was as if the carpet unrolled to cover about a quarter of the auditorium. Again, it was a strange spectacle, as about a quarter of those present were experiencing the actual presence of God while the rest were apparently unaffected. I kept saying that we must welcome the visitation of the Holy Spirit. Now, those halfway back in the hall started to do this. Those in front all turned round to see what was happening. I called out to them to turn again to the front and welcome what God was doing. Suddenly it appeared as if all 5,000 people were engaged with God simultaneously. It was as if the carpet had completed its unrolling.

That experience at New Wine mirrored another one I had had in Northern Ireland in the late 1970s. I had been there with one of our Faith Sharing Teams leading a series of meetings throughout the province. At the end of one meeting, I saw in my mind a wave beginning to break at the back of the hall. I knew that it was a wave of the Holy Spirit. As I saw it, I was overcome with a great sense of urgency. I knew somehow that if those present did not receive the Spirit's presence then they would miss what God had intended for them. By nature I am more of an introvert than an extrovert, but on this occasion I seized the microphone and implored those present to forget about themselves and call on the Holy Spirit. As I saw the wave break from the back of the hall and flood towards the front, I heard myself saying constantly, 'Receive! Receive!' After the wave had passed, I knew that for those who had not responded what God had intended was all over. At the end of this particular meeting, I invited people to share testimonies of what God had done. A number came forward. With great hesitancy, one lady told how she had been reluctant to respond to God at first. As the wave of the Spirit broke upon the meeting and she began to respond, her left leg, crippled at birth through polio, had returned to normal. Friends who had come with her confirmed that she had indeed been crippled and their joy in this work of healing was contagious. God had visited his people powerfully.

If God speaks through words and visions today, I also know that he can speak through dreams. Following my accident, I felt it was difficult for my emotions to deal with the trauma of the events I had been through. It was as if my emotions were like balloons attached to strings within me. Each needed to be cut and released. Prayer had the effect of releasing many of these painful emotions, but I found still others were released through dreams.

Dreams are a way of resolving the day's events and are natural to everyone, even if we do not always remember them. God, however, can use dreams as a way to speak to us. These could be termed 'significant dreams'. In the book of Job, Elihu expresses the matter as follows: 'For God does speak – now one way, now another – though a man may not perceive it. In a dream, in a vision of the night when deep sleep falls on men as they slumber in their beds' (Job 33:14–15).

Significant dreams can be received in different ways. Sometimes as soon as we wake the dream is remembered in vivid detail. I feel that with such a dream everything has significance. In Daniel chapter 2, Daniel not only tells Nebuchadnezzar the contents of a dream like this but then interprets every detail of it. Sometimes, though, on waking we cannot immediately remember having had a dream. It is often much later in the day when the dream is recalled. It was that sort of experience that Bob Jones had had when Mary and I met him in July 1990 and he was convinced that we had had a previous meeting and that he knew me quite well.

Some significant dreams are like silent movies; they flow from scene to scene and their interpretation is obvious. Others need interpreting, but interpreting dreams is a spiritual gift. Both Joseph and Daniel exercised this. I feel this gift is like that of the interpretation of tongues. It seems to be spoken 'from the lips', not the mind. Mary has this gift and as soon as she has heard a significant dream, she will say immediately what it means without apparently thinking about it. Sometimes I have had a dream and the interpretation has come through a scripture that I have heard spoken audibly during the dream. It is often the chapter and verse of a particular book.

Daniel seems to have discovered that it was important to write out his dreams: 'Daniel had dreams and visions passed through his mind as he was lying in bed. He wrote down the substance of his dreams' (Daniel 2:1).

Personally, I believe that after writing down our dream it is important that we ask a number of questions about what we have seen. The first one is to decide who the dream applies to. Sometimes it is God's way of speaking to his church or giving revelation concerning its present state. One year, immediately prior to the New Wine conference, I had five dreams on consecutive nights about the state of the church in England. If the dream concerns a local church then it is important that the dream is written out and given to the pastor concerned, along with its suggested interpretation.

Once a young married woman I knew appeared in a dream of mine. She seemed to be greatly depressed and I had the impression that she was contemplating suicide. She and her husband lived some distance away and I telephoned them to arrange a visit. When I visited her I did not feel that it would have been appropriate to mention the context of my dream, but as we talked the woman expressed how troubled and depressed she was and I was able to pray for her.

During this long period of immobilization I thought a lot

about the various ways God speaks to his church. As I thought about them I felt more and more convinced that God wanted to release more effectively the gift of prophecy to his church.

5
Moving Out

Seven long weeks after my accident, a change in my treatment was announced. Mr McCormick's team told me that I was to be fitted with a 'halo'. Fairly certain that this couldn't have had any spiritual significance, I left it to Gordon the registrar to explain what was meant. He explained that on the following morning they intended to fix what was technically called a halo traction unit on to my head. This was a metal ring fixed with four two-inch screws into my skull. After a few days, when this had settled into place, he would attach it by a frame to a chest corset so that with my neck now firmly immobilized I would at last be able to sit up and begin to walk again. The news filled me with both joy and dread in equal proportions.

The next morning Gordon arrived with a large package from America and with all the enthusiasm of a child with a Christmas gift unwrapped the halo for me to see. As he assembled the halo, I felt I could see fire all over it. Still delighted with the apparatus, Gordon prepared to start fixing it into my skull. I wondered if there was any danger that, in his evident enthusiasm, he would get carried away and end up putting the four screws into my brain. It was not an amusing thought. As he started to turn the first screw into my skull, I reminded myself of the promise that, whatever happened, it would not actually burn me, and forced myself to relax. The pain was searing and I caught my breath. 'When you walk through the fire, you will not be burned,' I repeated to myself again and again as the screws ground into bone.

Finally, the halo was fitted. As I tried to adjust to the extraordinary feeling of having my head contained in this way, I let the team fit the weights back on again. Then I settled back to the interminable routine of being turned every four hours.

A few days later Gordon and a colleague arrived with the corset. The moment that I had been praying about ever since I'd been told that there was the possibility of walking again had now arrived. I wondered whether those tedious and painful leg exercises had done any good. Carefully, the doctors sat me on the edge of the bed and fitted the corset to my halo. The hope was that, supported by the medical staff, I would be able to stand by the bedside. Slowly, I stood up. The combination of the corset and the halo was like a small bag of potatoes attached to me, making me feel top-heavy and unbalanced. Quivering, feeling that at any moment I would fall over, I cautiously stood upright. With infinite watchful care, the doctors and nurses slowly let go of me.

I was able to stand unaided!

Warily, I explored what was possible. The rigid corset fixed my upper body in a set position so that the only way I could turn was by making an action that involved my entire body. Encouraged and exhilarated by being upright at last after nearly two months in bed, I tried to move my feet. Painfully and unsteadily, I lifted them one by one. To the apparent astonishment of the medical staff I clumsily walked out of my room and down the ward! Only as I came to the wall at the far end did I realize that I could find no way to turn around that didn't involve the risk of falling over entirely. Eventually I invented an awkward shuffling movement that somehow allowed me to rotate. Returning to my room the staff helped me onto the bed, where I lay down completely exhausted, but my heart was full of praise and worship to God.

As I practised my new mobility over the next few days, I started to dare to think about returning to England, and I began to put pressure on the medical team to let me go home. The result was one of Mr McCormick's frank talks. There was no way, he told me firmly, that I could fly back to England with the halo on. Although my neck was healing, I was still in the very early stages of recovery and I would need medical supervision for some time to come. However, with some reluctance, he gave permission for me to stay somewhere near the hospital. I would be under the care of a nurse and I would have to return to the hospital for regular examinations and X-rays. My relief at the prospect of being able to leave the hospital ward was tempered by a sense that the next round of my battle of faith and fire was about to begin.

Following the conversation with Mr McCormick, Mary arranged to go with Andrew Smith, a local doctor, to find a suitable place for us to stay. Clearly this had to be near the hospital where they could continue to give support, but we also felt we needed pleasant surroundings after the sterile and barren environment of my hospital room.

As Mary left me, I felt myself sink almost physically into a pool of despair. Suddenly I felt terribly vulnerable. Here in hospital a magnificent medical team surrounded me. Help was always just a bell press away. Furthermore, although the corset allowed mobility of a sort I still had to be lifted up out of bed and lowered back down into it. Walking was still very difficult and I had a severe balance problem. I worried about what would happen if I fell out of bed and Mary was unable to lift me. Although I was desperate for a change of scenery

I was suddenly struck with doubts about leaving the protective cocoon of the hospital. Feeling very fragile, I felt assailed by doubts. My faith in God's ability to provide what I needed was strongly challenged. Did he really know everything? As I was telling the Lord my fears, he reminded me of a number of occasions in the past when he had wonderfully intervened for me.

Two remarkable incidents he brought to mind involved a gold ring engraved with a fish and a cross that Mary had given to me on our twenty-fifth wedding anniversary and which had become something that I treasured very much. The first incident had happened when leading a Bible school in northern Siberia one summer. I had gone one afternoon with the Faith Sharing Team to a local lake for a swim. As I got out of the water, I discovered to my dismay that the ring was missing from my finger. A sense of panic came over me and I immediately retraced my steps searching for it. Unable to find it, I simply prayed, 'Lord, I believe you know all things and that includes where my ring is.' When I returned to the flat where we were staying, there, lying on the table, was the ring. How it had got there involved an extraordinary story. To accommodate us an old lady had moved out of her traditional one-bedroom flat to stay with a daughter. Each day, however, she returned to the flat to dust it and put some food in the cupboard. On that particular day she had gone into the bathroom. Above the bath was a pump that took the water out to the main drainage system. She had never paid any attention to it before, but on this occasion she felt somehow compelled to unscrew the front. As she did so she found my ring lying at the bottom!

The second incident with the ring occurred a few months later when I was speaking in Lapland and Finland with my colleague James Roberts. After leading a conference in Oulu in northern Finland, we had flown to Helsinki, where I spoke to the leaders of the Bible Society and later that evening participated in a celebration in the famed wooden church in the centre of the city. As I stood up to speak after the worship session, I was horrified to discover that my ring was missing again. Very upset, I prayed immediately that the Lord would find it for me. After the meeting, I asked James if he would retrace our steps and see if he could find the ring. However, when we met up later in the evening he had to tell me that he had been to every place but had not found the ring. The following day, as I was sitting in the front seat of the car being taken to the airport, I prayed, 'Lord, I am leaving the country now without my ring. You know exactly where it is. Could you please return it?' I had just finished the prayer when James lent forward from the back of the car. Held between his fingers was my ring! He told me he had found it in a crack at the back of the rear seat, but how it got there remains a mystery as I had never once sat in the back of that car during our visit.

'Does God really know everything?' I had asked myself as I considered the future with concern. Reflecting on these incidents, I felt that God had given me these 'signs of the ring' in order that I might always know that nothing is impossible or too difficult for him. The level of my faith rose and now, calm and expectant, I was able to wait for Mary to come back.

When Mary returned to the hospital she brought the good news that she had found a suitable place and had booked us into a motor lodge called Harringtons. Harringtons had an ideal location. It was near the hospital and in pleasant surroundings, being directly opposite the Esplanade, the gardens that we had visited on the morning of the accident.

Despite this news and the reassurance of my recollections of the Lord's previous help, I still found the idea of moving out of the hospital highly nerve-racking. Practically, too, it was far from easy. Even getting into the car to travel to the motor lodge was a laborious process and fortunately

Andrew Smith, the doctor, came with us to help. Although I was firmly strapped into the front seat as we drove along I found myself terrified of being jolted. At the other end of our journey, climbing out of the car also proved difficult, with the heavy frame immobilizing my head and shoulders. On arrival at Harringtons, James and Jane O'Brien, the owners, welcomed us. Their warmth and concern did much to calm me as we settled into what was to be our home for several weeks. It later turned out that the O'Briens, whom we came to know well, were new to the motel business; James had moved to Palmerston North after years of sheep farming. Jane had been an English teacher, was very artistic, and had chosen beautiful furnishings and fabrics, something that I deeply appreciated after the functional decor of the hospital. I was also delighted to find that not only was our room attractively furnished but it was also well equipped. In particular, there was a bath with a spa. With the halo and corset structure that extended down to my lower chest, showering was out of the question. But taking a bath might be possible.

Now, with Mary as my main carer, we started to settle into a daily routine that was gruelling for both of us. Every day I would wake up feeling as if a sack of heavy potatoes were pressing on my neck. As I lay there with my head pressed down onto the pillow, I would rehearse in my mind every detail of how I was going to get up. When I had done that I would take a deep breath and start to get out of bed.

First of all, I would swing my legs over the bed and place them on the floor. Then, with Mary's help and a firm act of the will, I would lift my upper body into the vertical position. The moment I did this the whole room would begin to spin as if I were on a merry-go-round. Just as I wanted to vomit, the rotation of the room would slow down and some sort of equilibrium would be regained. Unsteadily I would make my way to the dining area.

The next event was breakfast, which Mary prepared.

Because my head was fixed so that I could only look straight ahead, I could not actually see what I was eating. This meant that Mary had to direct the food into my mouth. This had many hilarious moments and often there was more food on the floor than on my plate.

After breakfast, we started the bathroom ritual. The district nurse had provided steps that fitted into the bath. Using them, I would slowly edge my way into the bath by first sitting on the top step and then cautiously lowering myself down onto the next step until I was right in the water. Only then could I relax in the swirling waters. Getting out was equally laborious. The whole process made me so tired that I regularly had to sit down until I was dried and the last piece of clothing had been put on me.

From the moment of getting up until I had finished being dressed in my shorts and large shirt took two hours. At the end of it, I would feel emotionally and physically exhausted, and Mary would lower me onto the sofa. There, with pillows to support me, I would slowly regain my strength.

Now on the sofa we would read the Bible and pray together, something we have always sought to do regularly throughout our married life. The pattern we have found helpful has been to work through one Bible book at a time and, having read the allocated chapter, to share the thoughts that have come from it and turn these into praise, thanksgiving and intercession. Now, in this strange setting, we continued this pattern.

During these weeks it seemed that what I most needed was comfort. One passage that spoke to me about this was one that Paul wrote in 2 Corinthians: 'Praise be to the God and Father of our Lord Jesus Christ, the Father of compassion and the God of all comfort who comforts us in all our troubles, so that we can comfort those in any trouble with the comfort we ourselves have received from God' (2 Corinthians 2:3–4).

I discovered that the comfort of God came to me in many ways. After our reading and prayers, the telephone usually started to ring with calls from friends in England. A number always telephoned at the same time and day each week. My close friends Chris Hughes and James Roberts phoned frequently and Tim Watson, an old friend from theological college, phoned every week. Shirley and Arthur Hartup often phoned Mary. St Andrew's Church most generously financed the calls from our family, which enabled them to phone us often. The words they spoke were always comforting and encouraging, and I usually found that I came off the phone in floods of tears.

Next, the postman would arrive, often bearing cards, letters and tapes of recorded books. A number of children sent me drawings. Some were entitled 'Barry on the wave' and often had a drawing of an enormous blue wave, with me either walking on the top or swimming madly on the side. Their parents sent encouraging Bible verses or told how, in difficult circumstances, the Lord had comforted them. I discovered that deep thoughts and feelings could be expressed through letters. Mary put the correspondence in a large basket and I was able to reread many of the letters many times.

Most weeks, there were flowers and many other gifts. One morning the biggest hamper I have ever seen was carried into our lounge. James and Jane were equally excited about its arrival and came in to watch it being opened. They sat on the floor with Mary as she pulled out the contents: packets of steaks, fruit, vegetables, chocolates, champagne and wine. There seemed to be double of everything and Mary laid it all out on the floor and divided it in two. We realized that the giver had indicated that his gift symbolized a double blessing that the Lord intended to bestow upon us. We were overwhelmed and decided immediately to give half away so that the blessing we had received would also bless others. Mary gave out small food parcels to people from the local church who had helped us, and we arranged a small dinner party with James and Jane, who dressed for the occasion. When we eventually left for England they still had some steaks left in their freezer!

Another source of divine comfort came from the staff of Palmerston North Community Church who visited us regularly. Their kindness was overwhelming. They provided a car and petrol coupons for Mary and had our cupboard filled with groceries.

One strange and special comfort came in connection with a rugby match. When Frazer, who led the church, heard I was interested in rugby, he said that he would try and get some tickets for a Tri-Nations match. These turned out to be unobtainable, however, as the game had been sold out for some weeks. Nevertheless, we discovered that if I went in a wheelchair, I could join the area reserved for the handicapped. Mary was able to hire a chair from the Medical Aids Department in Palmerston North and on the day Frazer duly arrived and lifted me into his car. Arriving at the ground he transferred me to the wheelchair and, with the help of others, pushed me up to the place allocated. As he did, I saw that many other people in wheelchairs, some of whom were severely handicapped, surrounded me. Sitting there I suddenly felt very vulnerable and realized what other people must feel like when this is their only form of mobility. I enjoyed every minute of that evening and the next day watched the replay on TV. Just behind where I was seated had been a number of young people with cow bells and whenever their team scored they rang the bells and the TV cameras panned onto them. Each time they did this, I was fascinated to see myself in the midst of the wheelchairs.

In his second letter to the Corinthians the apostle Paul recounted how he had been comforted by the coming of his friend and colleague, Titus:

> For when we came into Macedonia, this body of ours had no rest, but we were harassed at every turn – conflicts on the outside, fears within. But God, who comforts the downcast, comforted us by the coming of Titus, and not only by his coming but also by the comfort you had given him. (2 Corinthians 7:5–6)

This reminds us that God's comfort often comes to us through others who bring to us the things that we need to be comforted. In so many ways, we found that we were comforted and supported by the warmth of both the new friendships we had made and those of our old friends at home who remembered us daily.

After the morning routine, we would eat lunch and then have a rest. Then we would walk across the road to the park. Initially, I felt this to be as daunting as climbing Mount Everest. I felt especially fearful crossing the road, as I was unable to walk very quickly and the cars came past at speed. Once safely in the park we would laboriously make our way past the duck ponds to the aviary of tropical birds. It was here that I discovered the Australian cockatoo. Over the weeks that I visited him, he learned to recognize my voice and would come when I called him. He would cling onto the wire cage and then stick his beak through a hole so that I could touch him and rub his chest. I derived enormous pleasure from the relationship we had and each morning would wake up eagerly anticipating being able to see him again. Recounting this now, my reaction seems exaggerated and even strange, but at the time I found that he was another source of God's comfort to me.

In addition to the friendly cockatoo, we also met Laura and Lee, who took care of the rose garden. Every day they would stop to talk with us and would often give us bunches of roses to take back to our room. They always encouraged us and eagerly looked forward with us to the day the halo would be removed. These walks were therapeutic in focusing me away from myself and the situation I was trapped in, but they also left me tired and uncomfortable. Under the fleece-lined corset, the heat generated by the walk made my skin itchy and irritated. In an effort to bring relief to the inflamed area, Mary would soak flannels in iced water and push them up under the corset.

In addition to the physical burdens I faced it was at this time that I slowly became aware that I was not going to recover all my faculties. The doctors had always been optimistic and had told me that the bruised nerves could regain their function but that it would take time. Although I had been positive and full of hope, I now began to realize deep down that with some things nothing had improved since the accident and I began to wonder if some nerves had in fact been permanently damaged. I was still paralysed in my lower arms and in half my hands. The back of my eyes had been damaged when I was dumped on the sea bed and this had left me with blurred vision. Repeatedly the question came back to me: 'Will I ever be the same again?'

As I raised that question, I thought about the way God works. I was reminded of what he said through the prophet Isaiah: 'For my thoughts are not your thoughts, neither are your ways my ways' (Isaiah 55:8).

Through this time, I came to realize that we are not excluded from sufferings and difficulties but that God comes to us in them and, if we allow him, he will create his life in us through them. The first part of each Gospel describes miracles and the second describes suffering, and Jesus is with us in both. I had experienced miracles and now had experienced suffering. I learned that God speaks to us through both of them.

Six weeks passed, every day of which was marked by the gruelling routines imposed on Mary and me by the constraints of the halo. Although these routines were simple and became part of a regular ritual, I always found them demanding, physically and emotionally. The burden of them did at least encourage me to push the surgical team on to remove the halo traction and allow me to travel home.

Every week, Mary and I attended the hospital to see Mr McCormick and 'my boys', his registrars Rob and Gordon. Each time we visited, I hoped that he would give permission for the halo to be unscrewed. It was evident, though, that we had different agendas. He was cautious, seeing my situation through his decades of medical experience, while I, increasingly, was longing to be at home with our own children and our new adopted family. I wanted to sleep in my own bed.

My meetings with Mr McCormick would always start in relaxed informality. Then I would tell him that I felt that the Lord was probably saying that it was time for the halo to come off and for me to go home. Ever the master of such situations, Mr McCormick would simply reply in a quiet voice that all seemed to be going well and that he would review my progress again the following week. After the verdict had been delivered, I would glance in mute appeal to the registrars, hoping for their intervention. However, despite a great deal of sympathy, Mr McCormick remained sternly immovable. As the weeks dragged on and Mr McCormick still refused to allow me my freedom, I began to feel discouraged. Would I ever return home?

The morning Mr McCormick finally yielded and said that the halo traction could come off was an incredible one. We arrived at the hospital as usual and sensed something was in the air. But Mr McCormick gave nothing away, calmly performing his clinic as usual. The X-rays were scrutinized and we watched as different bones were illuminated on the screen. I noticed that Gordon was looking particularly excited and kept grinning at us. Rob appeared from behind a door where he was attending a patient, waved and vanished again. Finally, Mr McCormick came over, pulled the screens around our cubicle and made his announcement in calm, measured tones. Immediately Gordon arrived holding a spanner in his hand. With even more enthusiasm than he had fitted the screws, Gordon removed them. He then put them carefully in a pot, which he solemnly handed over to Mary to take home. It was a holiday souvenir with a difference!

As I sat there staring straight ahead, afraid to move, Gordon produced a large package. 'This is your new neck brace,' he told me. 'You will need to wear this for a few months before you have a soft collar.' Made of solid plastic, the brace protected my neck and held my head in a rigid position, with a hard cup supporting my chin. My head movement was still strictly restrained, but it was a tremendous relief to have the weight lifted from my head and to have the corset and frame removed.

I began to plan our flight home. Mr McCormick suggested we book a flight in a couple of weeks, to allow me to have one more hospital appointment. He warned me that although it had already been three months since the accident, I would still have to take a whole year off work and I could expect that any full recovery would take at least two years. I also had to be aware that there would still be an element of uncertainty over the lasting effects of such a severe accident.

Preparations for our return home occupied my waking hours for the next weeks. As we prepared to leave, we found we had acquired so many X-rays and hospital notes, as well as the encouraging letters and faxes, that Mary had to buy another suitcase. Even so, we had to leave the cards behind! Booking flights, seeing family and saying goodbye to all the friends we had made gave a heightened interest to our remaining days in New Zealand.

One minor hiccup occurred when the chest rash that had troubled me spread up under my chin and became so uncomfortable that it was necessary for Mary to arrange for me to have my beard shaved off. A local man who had been a mountaineer in the Himalayas performed this necessary task. I found that losing my beard strangely affected me; it seemed to have diminished me. James Roberts phoned from England to say that he had had a dream of me without my beard and he sensed that I felt humiliated.

The night before we left New Zealand James and Jane called us to show us a complete rainbow that had appeared over Harringtons. We took the promise of God's covenant to our hearts again as we prepared to return home on what was now a new and unknown path.

At the airport, friends from the church gathered to see us off and photographed us in front of an Air New Zealand poster. On it were written the words 'Riding the Storm'.

6
Trauma

Mary and I had an almost overwhelming welcome as we returned to our friends and family back in Chorleywood. But after all the tears and laughter of the reunions had died away, I began to face the future. I did not really believe the medical team from New Zealand with their talk of a year off work to recuperate and two years at least to be healed as far as I was going to be. After the euphoria of homecoming had worn off, I began to get extremely frustrated. I became bored and found myself suffering enormous mood swings. I longed to leave the accident behind and wanted to get on with my life. I had enjoyed an itinerant ministry for 25 years and wanted to get back on the road as soon as possible. During my absence, my friend and colleague James Roberts had either fulfilled my engagements personally or had organized others to do so. I now felt I wanted to take on some of them again.

Before my accident, I had accepted an invitation to preach in all the Welsh cathedrals. This had been a great honour and we had seen wonderful days of celebration and the visitation of the Spirit of God in these ancient centres of worship. Only St David's in Pembrokeshire remained outstanding, and five months after breaking my neck James and I set out to fulfil my commitment to preach there.

It took James five hours to drive to St David's, the smallest city in the United Kingdom. My new plastic neck brace forced me to stare straight ahead for the entire journey, and by the time we arrived I felt utterly drained. Although it was only late afternoon, I could not wait to lower myself into bed. I fell over in the bath and, at times, had to struggle to stay above the ample water line. Despite my exhaustion, I was determined to keep going.

In the cathedral the next day, one of our hosts took us to see a plaque that commemorated, in Welsh, the life of a parish priest. His dying prayer, recorded and dated 1903, was that God would revive the spiritual life in the principality. A year later, the Holy Spirit fell upon the churches in north and south Wales at the same time. As a result, Evan Roberts and others took the good news about Jesus throughout the nation. The zeal of these faithful men of God had been an encouragement to me for many years. I remembered discussing the 1904 visitation of God to Wales with a vicar 15 years earlier in north-east Wales. My host had taken down a book with tattered covers from his extensive library. Opening at a well-thumbed section he read me a passage that included a story that has stuck in my mind ever since. In 1904 a man from London, fascinated by the reports of the spiritual renewal that was occurring in Wales, took a train there to find out for himself what was happening. Crossing the border, he called the guard and asked where he should get off to encounter the revival. The answer he was given was that he would know as soon as the train moved into it. The idea of a region where the presence of God is so powerful that it is discernible by all who enter it has intrigued and challenged me ever since.

On the Saturday in St David's Cathedral, I preached on something that I had thought about while immobile on my bed in New Zealand. I had read that during Abraham's lifetime his servants had dug wells that had obviously been the source of life for his people and their livestock. However, after Abraham died the Philistines had blocked up all the wells, and other wells in Israel were unusable because of disputes and quarrels. When Abraham's son Isaac came into leadership it is recorded in Genesis 26:18 that he 'reopened the wells that had been dug in the time of his father Abraham, which the Philistines had stopped up after Abraham died, and he gave them the same names his father had given them'. Wells symbolize salvation. In Isaiah 12:3 we read of God telling his people, 'With joy you will draw water from wells of salvation.' Wells were also community centres, places where people socialized and where physical thirst was quenched. In Wales, I said, God had in the past created wells of his Spirit and the narratives of those revival days record many such places and many thousands who came to them to be made spiritually alive in Jesus. Since then enemies of the gospel had come and blocked up the wells. I have stood in front of a chapel where Evan Roberts had preached and as I did I held in my hand a book describing the revival that had come through his preaching. In front of me was a commemorative plaque that was polished regularly. The people, though, had long gone. As I preached I felt that I had travelled from a hospital bed in New Zealand to St David's Cathedral with the simple message that God wanted his people to take out of the life of his church those things that the enemy had put in, and when they did this they would discover wells of great spiritual life.

My return to preaching had been terribly draining. On my return to Chorleywood, I literally collapsed for a week and I could hardly move out of bed. On the one hand I wanted to return to normal life, but on the other something deep and painful was happening within me. I was later to realize that although I was still struggling to cope emotionally and physically, I was reluctant to give in to the obvious need to convalesce properly. I was desperate to regain something of my life as it had been before and began to search for a way forward. In that frame of mind, I remembered Sarawak.

Some years previously James Roberts and I had been invited to be speakers at a conference in Sarawak, North Borneo. This was organized by the Diocese of Kuching under the leadership of Bishop John Leong Chee Yun. We had gone for two weeks and in addition to speaking at the conference, we had spoken at the cathedral in Kuala Lumpur, led meetings at St Faith's Church and had preached in many villages. We had enjoyed days of great blessing, had seen the Holy Spirit meeting with church leaders in new ways and had been encouraged by the many who came to know Jesus for the first time. We had also seen people be physically healed and released from demonic torment. In one village, after being healed from deafness, the local witch doctor had confessed faith in Jesus. As I thought of those events, I remembered how many of the leaders had asked us at the time whether we would return. I had always made it a policy not to accept such an invitation, feeling that you never knew what the Lord might want of you in the year ahead. Now, though, I went to my files and retrieved the correspondence folder marked 'Malaysia'. This, I thought, would be a way ahead. James and I would return and have follow-up meetings. I quickly drew up an itinerary and faxed all the relevant people. Many replied saying that they would need to consult their leadership but thought that it was probably the wrong time of the year. I waited patiently as the official replies came in. They were all negative – something that had never happened to me before. The hope the idea had cultivated vanished. I was back to square one.

Then, however, another new way forward seemed to open up. In May 1997 I had felt that I heard the Lord say, 'My time has come for the cities.' As a result, I had made a study of the cities in the Bible and God's relationship to them. I thought of Jonah and his call to preach the gospel to the great pagan city of Nineveh. He had run away from God's call and yet through his experience of 'death and resurrection' in being swallowed and then spat out by the great fish, he had come to know God's power to bring a nation to repentance through his preaching. In Nineveh, the people had received his message with great repentance and turning to God. God had indeed changed that city. I had also been struck by the evident strategy of Paul to preach the gospel and create churches in the major cities of the Roman Empire. Before my accident, I had preached at St John's, Harborne, in Birmingham, where my friend John Hughes was the vicar. During the worship there, I saw a vision in which the walls of the church suddenly fell down like giant cards so that the worshippers could be seen by the people in the community around the church amid their Sunday shopping and socializing. With walls down there was a coming and going between those who worshipped the Lord and those who were in the group outside. I felt it meant that the gospel was coming to the city.

Encouraged by my memories of this, I made contact with John, who arranged a meeting for leaders in the city to hear me speak on 'God's plans for the cities'. A relatively small group gathered at the largest church to hear me speak on God's heart for the city and its people. The vision I had had was so real to me that I thought it would ignite in the hearts of those who heard me. The response was encouraging, but I returned home tired and exhausted.

A further reason for discouragement at this time was the fact that it had been wrongly reported in a number of articles that because of my accident I was no longer able to be involved with the New Wine conferences. In fact, as I have written earlier, I had actually resigned in Easter 1996, well before my accident. These reports had the effect of drastically slowing down the invitations for me to preach and minister with teams. Many people thought that as a result of my accident I had taken early retirement. In fact I had a number of letters thanking me for my ministry and wishing me well in retirement. This all worked very much against me and seemed to frustrate my desire to return to my old level of activity. I now see that I was in fact finding it difficult to accept that God was providing space in my diary for me to regain strength and healing, and that I was actually fighting against this.

Based on St Andrew's, Mark Stibbe had organized a conference on revival and had asked Ken and Lois Gott from Sunderland and J. John the evangelist to speak with him. To my surprise, Mark asked me over lunch one day to share with the conference what had happened to me in New Zealand and what I was learning from it. When I spoke at the conference I found it a very loving and sympathetic gathering. Many of the delegates and their churches had prayed for us and contributed to the incredible numbers of letters, cards, tapes, telephone calls and drawings Mary and I had received in New Zealand. In this atmosphere, I was able to be very vulnerable and honest. The sharing of my story was continuously interrupted with tears.

After I returned home that evening, I sat by myself and considered the events of the afternoon. I realized two things. The first thing was the fact that although I had spoken in considerable personal weakness, the Holy Spirit had been present in power. I saw that through the accident I had been reduced to a total dependency on the resources of the Holy Spirit alone. I had invited for prayer those who were experiencing suffering in their lives because of situations they were unable to understand, and it seemed as if God had come powerfully to many, not necessarily to answer their questions, but to meet with them in their situations.

The second thing I realized was that I was still suffering from serious trauma. The results of trauma are probably the least understood of all psychological conditions. For many years, the medical profession didn't seem to take such abnormal behavioural patterns particularly seriously. But this attitude is changing, as things like Post Traumatic Stress Disorder are now widely recognized.

As I considered my own continuing trauma and how best to deal with it, I was reminded of an incident that occurred in my youth. One of my great joys as a teenager was horse riding and although I never owned my own horse, I always had the use of one. I used to enjoy taking horses over the jumps. On one occasion I was working a young horse, and all went well until she came to a particularly high jump that she was obviously afraid of. She baulked at this and, more than once, I found myself catapulted at speed over the hurdle to a hard landing on the other side. In my attempts to make her leap the hurdle, I would bring her back again and again, trying to tell her through my body language that all was well and that she had nothing to fear. Finally, I persuaded her to jump and once over safely I immediately made her repeat the hurdle again so that her confidence would grow.

As I thought of this, I suddenly realized that there were many hurdles of trauma that I had not been able to face. As I approached them, the pain became too much and I baulked at them. I would find other ways to cope with them and other things to divert my attention away from facing the pain. For example, I would go and watch the TV or turn on the radio. Somehow I realized that I would have to stop these avoidance tactics.

In an effort to help myself, I started to name the hurdles. The terrible moments in the waves were an obvious focus for the trauma. The feelings I had experienced there had been overwhelming: losing all control, being completely in the hands of the elements, being tossed savagely by the sea, feeling suffocated and finally slipping into unconsciousness and thinking it was death. It was all still very real to me.

Another hurdle was my memory of Mr McCormick sitting

by me describing in detail the imminent surgery; the description of what my future life would be if the operation went wrong. Over and over again I could hear him say, 'Because of the location of the injury, the X-rays have been inconclusive. When I open you up I don't know what I might find. You could wake up paralysed from the neck down.' Murray's description shortly after of how he would insert his tubes and make incisions to anaesthetize me was another related hurdle, as was the morning of the operation itself – being wheeled into the operating theatre and realizing that my future mobility was in the hands of those who were greeting me.

Even my gradual regaining of consciousness had involved an intense but brief trauma as I had wondered whether I would return to my family as a quadriplegic. I remembered how my numb, unfeeling hands had gradually slipped across my stomach to my thighs until the sensation of the weight of my hands on my legs had told me that the operation had been a success.

There had been further hurdles. Being turned every four hours on a striker bed with its attendant giddiness and being totally dependent in the process on those who turned me; the fitting of the halo traction unit with the screws penetrating into my skull; learning to walk again and losing my balance as I did and lying helplessly on the floor waiting for someone to help me to my feet; lying in bed in the darkened ward, raging in pain and frustration as I failed to summon a nurse to give me painkillers.

I saw that although the word of God that had promised me that when I walked through the fire I would not be burned had given me hope and courage, it had not, in itself, stopped me from being affected by trauma. I also realized that these, and many more such experiences, had been like hurdles to me which up until now I had baulked at and not faced. Now I saw that God was challenging me to face up to them.

The challenge of facing up to my hurdles was made more difficult by the fact that Mary and I were having to face change in the church. In New Zealand we had looked forward so much to returning to our family, home and the people at St Andrew's. We had not been disappointed; our people were magnificent and at times we had found their genuine love almost overwhelming. However, in our three-month absence everything had changed. A new vicar and associate vicar had been appointed. The heart of the church as we had known it for a quarter of a century would, we knew, never be the same again. We had left for New Zealand with certain known and proven structures in place. We had returned to a different vision, and new structures had emerged. We wondered how I would fit into this. I think that after so many years these changes would have been stressful for me anyway. As they coincided with my return home with my own deep and unresolved trauma from the accident, they accentuated my insecurity.

Perhaps if we had been able to go somewhere new it would have been different. Certainly our desire had been to move on to a new ministry, but with my accident and the responsibility we had for our newly adopted family we had to stay where we were for the foreseeable future. But, I asked myself, if God did want me to stay on, what did he want me to do? Mark had given me the responsibility for 'outside ministries'. While this was a challenge, it pulled me away from the centre of the church and reduced my involvement in it. I felt that this was something of a bereavement, and it gave me the sense of being cut loose but unsure of where I should be heading.

Home too was not without its problems. My own issues were paralleled by the fact that our new family – Dylan, Tasha, Bruce and Bianca – were also starting to face up to their own intense traumas. It was only seven months since an after-supper row between their parents had resulted in their mother's death. Subsequently, they had lost their father through a violent death so that in just over a year they had lost both parents and their family home. They too were coming to the hurdles and finding that because of the pain they were unable to deal with them. I found that I was to have almost as much a ministry inside our home as outside it.

The delay that there was before trauma struck puzzled me at first. In the end, I realized that the body handles the initial trauma of loss by effectively anaesthetizing us, rather like a dentist before a tooth extraction. It is only later, when the anaesthetic fades, that the pain comes.

Another image that I found helpful was that of earthquakes. Growing up in New Zealand, they were a regular experience. A quake will dramatically shake an area, but after it has happened there may still be a long and alarming period of aftershocks, some of which may be nearly as powerful as the original shock. Traumas express themselves in a similar way as psychological shock waves continue to pass through the emotions long after the main event itself has passed. These aftershocks manifest themselves in a repetition of the feelings associated with the initial triggering event and can include feelings such as panic, fear and terror. At times, these trauma 'aftershocks' can be overwhelming in intensity. The same psychological shock waves also ripple through our minds, generating questions such as, 'Why should this have happened to me?' and 'Why would a loving, kind God allow me to go through such trauma and loss?'

One result of this effect is that day-to-day life, long after events such as accidents or bereavements, can become difficult as traumatic aftershocks can occur suddenly for little or no apparent reason. What happened to Mary is a good example. In New Zealand, she went into what she termed 'nursing mode' from the moment of the accident, forcing her professionalism to overrule her natural emotional responses to the sufferings I was going through. As a result, she appeared to have come through the whole thing remarkably unscathed. Months after the accident we were at home with friends, watching international rugby on the television. Abruptly the game stopped as one of the forwards received an injury. Instead of taking him to the sideline for attention he was left on the field and various medical personnel were summoned. After a while the commentator remarked that the injured player might well have broken his neck. As he said this, Mary started to scream, shake and weep uncontrollably with fear. Our friends and I gathered around her, and in prayer put the power of the cross between her and the effects of the trauma. As we did, the power of something was obviously broken and, after a little time, peace came to her. Clearly these waves of trauma can be unpredictable.

Most preachers who seek to be open with Jesus are usually quite transparent to their hearers. If they have unresolved areas of trauma in their own lives they will often use them as illustrations in their sermons until the trauma is eventually resolved. Resolution of trauma by retelling an event is particularly common with those who have been bereaved. I have often sat with bereaved people and listened to them. They frequently tell the story of the discovery of the death of their loved one, often recounting the loss in minute detail. I regularly used to visit an elderly lady whose husband had died after they had been married 40 years. Eventually I knew the story surrounding his death by heart and once, when she forgot a detail as she retold it for me again, I was able to remind her of it. Finally, a time came in my periodic visits when she no longer referred to her husband's death. It seemed to me that her traumatic loss was like a storm that had eventually blown itself out.

Although this telling and retelling of the events surrounding a trauma is a major ingredient to the healing, initially the need to talk about it can become almost obsessive. As I started to travel a little and speak again after my return to England, I always told my story. When the summer came, I was invited to speak at Home Focus, which is Holy Trinity Brompton's annual conference. For this I had prepared a talk that I entitled 'Bridges to Babylon', borrowing my title from a Rolling Stones CD and video. My theme was that ancient Babylon symbolized our modern culture with its bridges into seduction, materialism and New Age practices. In my conclusion, I wanted to show how through his death on the cross, where he broke the power of all that ancient Babylon symbolized, Jesus had made a bridge *from* Babylon. It was a message that I felt very strongly about, but late in the afternoon before I was to give my talk I decided once again to tell my story. In some ways this was almost a compulsive act, yet with each retelling of it something of the trauma's destructive power ebbed away from within me. It was as if it was a raging storm that slowly but eventually died out. One day I went to speak at a conference and found that I no longer felt a compulsive need to tell my story. I realized that in this particular area of my life I had indeed been healed.

Yet even if I had now come to terms with the pain and suffering of my ordeal, there was another area of my life in which I needed deep healing. In many traumas, there is not just the infliction of pain but also some sort of loss. The result is a grieving for something that, in this life at least, will never be restored. This is most obvious in bereavement, but the process also occurs in situations where relationships and physical conditions have been unalterably changed. This often means seeking to reconcile the person we are now with the person we once were. This is something that only God can really do for us.

For me I must accept that the person I am now is very different from the person I was before the accident. Now I am without feeling in my neck, parts of my arms and all but the thumb and forefinger of my hands. My eyesight is impaired, as the jolt on the back of my head when the wave dumped me on the sea floor somehow damaged the back of my eyes. My balance is affected, especially when I rise from a horizontal position. To maintain freedom of movement in my neck area I need to exercise at least twice a week in the gym, otherwise it starts to seize up.

Since the accident, I have been able to face up to what happened and to work through the traumas. I believe they are behind me. As a result, I am now starting to respond to God's calling on my life again. As I do, I see that the ministry the Lord is starting to restore me to is far removed from the one I once knew. I wonder perhaps if what I face now is a little like being called by Jesus to come to him walking on the water. Once I was sure and confident about so many aspects of the work of God's Spirit. I knew how to do it. What I face now though is new; I have never walked on water before.

As I face the challenges ahead, I am finding it necessary to spend time humbly waiting on and listening to God. Perhaps having had everything taken from me by God is a prophetic symbol for all who will be involved in the coming harvest.

7
A Parallel Storm?

In the enforced period of rest that I had now been given, I had plenty of time to reflect. These reflections were not only on my own situation but also on that of the church I knew and loved so well, St Andrew's, Chorleywood. As I considered the church in which I had spent so many happy years, as well as other English Churches, I felt that the situation in which it now found itself had strange parallels with what had happened to me. Was my own crisis prophetically symbolic of what they were going through? In order for me to explain why I thought this, I need to sketch out something of the remarkable history of St Andrew's, Chorleywood.

The parish of St Andrew's, Chorleywood, is a small community of approximately 7,500 people in Hertfordshire, 25 miles from the centre of London and on the northwestern edge of the M25 motorway that encircles London. Planning regulations stopped the creation of large housing developments in the area and in many ways the old village has been preserved. One part of the village has a pre-war council housing estate fairly near the church. Extending away in the other direction are a series of small hills on which private housing, some of it very expensive, has been built for a much more middle-class population.

The first St Andrew's church building was erected in 1908. After a start in a local pub, it then moved to a little corrugated iron building that became affectionately known as 'the tin tabernacle'. This stood where the present church hall stands today. In 1966, John Perry came as Vicar to lead a small congregation. In the late 1960s this group of worshippers had a visitation of the Holy Spirit as part of the charismatic renewal that was experienced by many churches worldwide. New life flowed into the church. The way people worshipped God changed: tradition was replaced with contemporary liturgy and a worship group led the congregation in new songs. The sick were prayed for with a new faith and, as a result, many people announced that they had been healed. People heard God speak and relayed this to the congregation in prophetic utterances. During the week, people began to meet in each other's homes to read the Bible, worship and pray together. One result of this renewal was that people began to respond financially by taking tithing seriously, and a decision was made to give away half the annual income. The changes were symbolized in the way the tin tabernacle was replaced by a modern building.

These changes were still underway when I joined St Andrew's as a curate in 1971. It was as part of this renewal that shortly after arriving I started the Faith Sharing Ministry. This was as a direct result of a vision that the Holy Spirit gave me in which, after a series of graphic pictures, the word came to me that we should take what we had experienced in the church to our community, the British Isles and on into the wider world. As a result of invitations, our teams started to travel throughout the United Kingdom and later extended their ministry to Europe and beyond. Each year, we invited representatives from the churches we had visited to a weekend that we hosted at home. Through these and other ventures, St Andrew's gradually became well known and a centre of the renewal movement. We were featured in many articles in papers and magazines, including the *Reader's Digest*.

In the middle of the 1970s David Pytches came to lead the church. David had been a missionary bishop in Chile, South America. He was a courageous pioneer and brought with him a large vision of God. A key point in David's ministry was when in 1981 he invited John Wimber and a team to visit the church at Pentecost. John, then little known in Britain, had discovered a truth about the Holy Spirit that had transformed his life and ministry and which was to lead to the creation of the worldwide chain of churches known as the Vineyard churches. John's discovery was that Jesus' saying in Luke 11:13, 'How much more will your Father in heaven give the Holy Spirit to those who ask him', was applicable, not only to an individual, but also to a congregation.

That Pentecost weekend and subsequently, after John Wimber had taught us from the word of God, he asked us to stand and invited the Holy Spirit to come and minister to us. John's simple request, 'Come, Holy Spirit', followed by a time of waiting, brought dynamic results. Some people were overwhelmed and collapsed onto the floor where they lay in a sleep-like state, sometimes for over an hour, in what came to be known as 'carpet time'. Many people later testified to the powerful presence of Jesus bringing peace and healing to them through this. Others found themselves shaking or experiencing heat as the Holy Spirit came upon them. The power of God was so present that there were reports of non-believers coming to faith.

It was a wonderful time and our eyes were opened to the truth that, through a simple invitation, the Holy Spirit could be allowed to work in our lives. John was always very concerned not to act on his own ideas but to listen to what he felt God was saying. One evening at St Andrew's he said that he believed God was anointing people with gifts of healing. Those who experienced heat in their hands were invited to go to the front where John and his team prayed for them. Those who went forward told later how the heat they had originally felt increased in intensity as they were anointed with oil and prayed over. During these times of affirming and imparting gifts, words of revelation would be spoken over the recipients. Many of our people also heard God speak to them. As they ministered these words to others, they had the joy of seeing the Holy Spirit at work, releasing his life into their lives.

Once John and his team had gone, David began to analyse what had happened. It was apparent that many people had experienced Jesus in new ways. These ranged from knowing the love of God, to the releasing of painful emotions and the healing of past traumas. Beyond the Holy Spirit meeting a person in his or her own inner life there had also been the anointing and empowering to bring the life of Jesus to others through prayer and the laying on of hands. David rapidly sought to harness what had happened. Those anointed with healing gifts were invited, along with those who had compassion and a desire to pray for the sick, to attend a training meeting. Over a series of weeks, David taught them what he had learned from John Wimber about ministering in the power of the Holy Spirit, and they became authorized members of the ministry team at St Andrew's. After each service, members of this team became available to pray with people and minister to their needs. David put the wisdom he had learned in a book entitled *Come, Holy Spirit* which has become something of a textbook for those developing such ministries.

Under David's leadership, St Andrew's quickly became one of the major centres for this new move of the Holy Spirit. On the basis that the Pentecostal revival in Azusa Street, Los Angeles, in 1906–8 was the first wave of a new work of the Holy Spirit and the charismatic renewal of the 60s was the second wave, some people have termed this new move the Third Wave. On Saturday evenings, crowds came to the celebration-type meetings with an enormous hunger for God. These meetings would involve worship, biblical preaching and people sharing their new experience of Jesus. Afterwards the Holy Spirit would be invited to come, and as people began to respond to his presence, the ministry team would pray for them. These meetings became so crowded that other centres were opened throughout the London area.

Regular Saturday conferences were organized to teach people how to minister effectively in the power of the Holy Spirit. By now, many church leaders wanted to introduce this sort of ministry to their own congregations and came with groups of people from their churches. Partly to meet the demand for leadership teaching in this area, midweek conferences for clergy were arranged and became so popular that the St Andrew's church database had a register of 2,000 leaders who had attended. Well-known American pastors would come to teach us at these meetings using their insights and experiences, while a growing number of English clergy came, telling of how they had introduced this ministry to their congregations.

An extension of all that was happening through the conferences and celebrations centred on our church was a series of conferences that David started at Swanwick for church leaders. These soon became so popular that they always had a waiting list. Realizing that more room was needed for people who wanted to attend, David decided to start a family holiday conference at the Royal Bath and West Showground at Shepton Mallet. This became known as the New Wine family conference and soon grew, so that today there are three such annual conferences, with many thousands of people attending. Initially our church ran the whole conference. We had a ministry team that had grown to 250 and many of them were on duty during the New Wine week, while other members of our congregation did most of the jobs on site.

David led New Wine, appointing Mike Pilavachi as his youth leader. Initially the meetings with young people took place during the main conference week, but this work too began to grow. As it rapidly expanded, it was decided to create another independent conference, which came to be called Soul Survivor. As with the previous ventures, this too grew quickly. Matt Redman, the musical director at St Andrew's, became the worship leader at Soul Survivor, and Matt's songs soon became very popular in many British churches.

Back at St Andrew's itself the congregation was growing. As it did, David started to challenge people who travelled to us from other areas to consider leaving to start churches in other towns or villages. This practice was pioneered within our own Anglican parish where for many years we had tried – with only limited success – to attract people from the council estate to our predominantly middle-class congregation. The new venture, the Chorleywood Christian Fellowship, was a breakthrough, and a number of previously unchurched people started to attend. On the other side of our parish, another group started up a church in the premises of a local school. This too became established and started to grow.

Controversy was inevitable when a number of people from the Watford area who had been visiting St Andrew's on a regular basis were challenged to start their own church. Watford, six miles away, fell in another Anglican parish and the church plant caused some consternation among the local clergy and the diocesan bishop. The issue was widely reported in the local and national press. No sooner had this church been set up than another fellowship was created in Watford – a youth church which came to be called Soul Survivor. Many young people were attracted to this church with its innovative expressions of worship. St Andrew's continued to pastor these churches, as well as another new church plant in Chesham.

Yet another new venture came about with the arrival of Teddy Saunders, a retired Anglican clergyman who moved to Chorleywood with his wife Margaret. They both had a great pastoral concern for clergy and church leaders, and their home, 'Hensol' in Shire Lane, became the venue for ten-day retreats to refresh and encourage Christian men and women in leadership. Delegates stayed in local homes and met for seminars in 'Hensol'. As news spread, leaders came not only from the UK but from Europe and other parts of the world. For many, these courses were life-changing and the spiritual renewal that they experienced reaped benefits within their own churches.

The result of all this activity was that, unwittingly, we all became well known. We became known through all our conferences and initiatives; teams travelled to the nations and there were appearances on TV and radio. I spoke in various regional celebrations; a number of the St Andrew's staff wrote books; Matt Redman's worship songs became widely sung in renewed churches and conferences. We had become well known across a large sector of the British church.

There were odd hints that this fame might be dangerous. When being welcomed by the deans of the various cathedrals I visited, I found myself surprised when a number made comments along the lines of, 'Of course, we think of St Andrew's as being a diocese within the St Albans Diocese.' Although meant as a joke, I found myself reflecting on this and beginning to feel uncomfortable. When a former bishop and his wife repeated the same comment over lunch in our home, I started to wonder whether perhaps the church was growing too important.

In July 1996 David Pytches left and it became my task to lead St Andrew's through the interregnum as we awaited Mark Stibbe's arrival. As I prepared for it, my mind went over the strange and little-understood process of change within churches. Little, if anything, has been written about the way churches change. A church is a unique organization and has little in common with a business or company when it comes to change. In those organizations you can hire and fire unit leaders, close down sections, combine or replace structures. Churches are different.

This was brought home to me when I came to St Andrew's in 1970 to replace John Hughes as the curate. Now the vicar of St John's, Harborne, in Birmingham, John is one of my best friends and we have happy memories of playing rugby together at college. However, replacing him led Mary and me to the most difficult year of our lives up to that time. For one thing, the leadership of the large youth group at St Andrew's had anticipated that everything was going to proceed as it had always done during the previous four years, with positions and responsibilities unchanged. For another, they had also assumed that I would be an exact replica of John. John and I, however, were different people, and my response to issues was much more intuitive and spontaneous. The changeover, then, was far from easy. I sensed that similar difficulties were to occur now. After all, all leaders establish a framework through which they can exercise leadership, and vicars are no different. A vicar selects lay people he is comfortable with and who, in his opinion, are equipped to further his vision for the work. David had done no more than that. The problem was that in St Andrew's such people had had an extraordinarily high profile that involved extensive travel and conference speaking, both in the UK and abroad.

As I thought about the future of our church, I found myself with the same uneasy sense I had had about my own future the day the Kansas City prophets had spoken over Mary and me at Holy Trinity Brompton. I felt deep inside me that the church was about to go into uncharted waters with God. I seemed to sense that what we had built up together and come to rely on would be taken down, and that God was going to use the coming change to inaugurate this.

One of my last talks to the church before we left for New Zealand was on preparing for change. It seemed important to me to prepare the congregation for the changes that would be inevitable under Mark's leadership, and I sought to point out that Mark would have his own vision for the church. He would, I implied, invite into his inner circle those whom he trusted and felt comfortable with. The result would be that many of us who had enjoyed a high-profile role in the past might no longer be called upon to have one in the new era. Obviously, I pointed out, our gifts would be used, but in different ways. After I had spoken about this, a number of the congregation thanked me. However, I knew the reality was going to be much more painful than my words had indicated.

When Mary and I returned home after the accident, I could see that Mark indeed had no intention at all of being a replica of David Pytches. Prior to being invited to consider the position at St Andrew's, he had felt independently that God was calling him to be its new leader. When he came to us from a three-month sabbatical, much of which had been spent in a Swedish theological college, Mark arrived with his own vision from God. That vision did not extend to automatically sustaining and developing what had already been accomplished. Uncertainty, change and storms were about to break.

Matt Redman's talented leadership of the worship had been close to the heart of the renewal at St Andrew's. I first came to know Matt the night after his father tragically died, when I took him and his older brother away for the day with our three children. Matt has come through a deep valley of suffering and I remember well the moving moment when, as a young teenager, he recited a poem on fatherhood at our evening worship. It described the suffering he had been through and the hope he knew in Jesus. Soon his poems were accompanied by music. Matt brought to St Andrew's a rare quality of song-writing: his songs had great depth and his leadership had a quality that was much respected. Despite the attention he received, Matt retained a genuine humility. Under Matt's inspiration, the worship of our church was transformed. A truly anointed worship leader can bring a congregation into the presence of God in such a way that the presence and power of the Spirit of God is the only focus. People journeyed for many miles just to be able to be part of such a service of worship led by Matt.

As Mark arrived, Matt left to join Mike Pilavachi at Soul Survivor, Watford. With him gone, the process of change gained pace. People started to leave our church. Suddenly a whole layer of the congregation moved away. Dozens of young couples with small children moved to join Soul Survivor at Watford. Within weeks, we lost what felt like an irreplaceable generation of gifted leaders, including many musicians and singers who had been brought together under Matt's leadership. Still others left to return to their local churches or moved on to other fellowships. There was an incredible shaking, which touched the very foundations of the fellowship.

What had happened? As I reviewed the situation, I felt that there was a parallel with my own accident. In hindsight, I now see that among those of us involved in St Andrew's, Chorleywood, there had been a subtle shift from building a kingdom for Jesus to building kingdoms for our own individual ministries. It had happened imperceptibly. I felt ashamed of my own part in it, recalling again how the Lord had challenged me through that account in the Gospels of how James and John had wanted visibility and even cosmic recognition. The veiled answer they had received was that indeed the cup and baptism of suffering would be theirs. Jesus, I feel, wanted to tell them that suffering was essential to break them out of their own human kingdoms and release them into his kingdom.

I believe that in the terrible moment I experienced in the wave, Jesus broke more than my physical neck. The neck in Scripture can symbolize arrogance and self-centredness. This is why, nearly 20 times in the Old Testament, God referred to his people as being 'stiff necked'. The implication was that they were set in their own plans and purposes.

I believe that in a similar way to that in which God worked so dramatically in my life, he also works in churches that consciously or unconsciously create a kingdom within his kingdom. In the 1980s I often heard John Wimber say, with deep feeling and conviction, that God wanted his church back. In my spirit I felt that a time of suffering would be coming to the church, and that St Andrew's would not be exempt from this. Although there would be a high personal cost it would enable the redirection of the church into a path of humble service.

It seemed important to me to reflect again on St Andrew's Church, its foundations and development to the present time. What was God saying? What was he tearing down in order that we could reflect his kingdom?

At the end of his letter to the Hebrew Christians, the author writes that the nature of God is to shake things for his own purposes:

> At that time his voice shook the earth, but now he has promised, 'Once more I will shake not only the earth but also the heavens.' The words 'once more' indicate the removing of what can be shaken – that is, created things – so that what cannot be shaken may remain. Therefore, since we are receiving a kingdom that cannot be shaken, let us be thankful, and so worship God acceptably. . . . (Hebrews 12:26–28)

This scripture reflects on the giving of the Law to Moses at Mount Sinai. On that occasion, the voice of God literally shook the earth. Yet through Haggai the prophet (whose words are quoted in verse 26), the Lord foretold a time when he would shake not only the earth but the heavens also. It is a reference to a shaking of both a physical and spiritual reality. When God acts in this way, what remains after the shaking are only those works that have an eternal value and they cannot be shaken because they belong to the kingdom of God.

Such shaking, when much of what we have relied upon is taken from us, is very painful. Jeremiah the prophet had a personal prophetic word for his secretary, Baruch, at a time when God was shaking his people and Baruch was feeling the pain of it:

> This is what the LORD, the God of Israel, says to you, Baruch: You said, 'Woe to me! The LORD has added sorrow to my pain; I am worn out with groaning and find no rest.'
>
> The LORD said, 'Say this to him [Baruch]: "This is what the LORD says: I will overthrow what I have built and uproot what I have planted, throughout the land. Should you then seek great things for yourself? Seek them not. For I will bring disaster on all people, declares the LORD, but wherever you go I will let you escape with your life."' (Jeremiah 45:2–5)

I am convinced that it is through these painful and traumatic processes that God creates a more humble and dependent people. Only such people can be his servants, entrusted with bringing in the harvest.

8

Facing Suffering and Death

Stretched out immobile on my hospital bed recovering from the accident, it was inevitable that my thoughts should turn to the problems of suffering and death. In my ministry I had grappled with them time and time again. Now, though, personally affected by intense suffering and with my imminent death a real possibility, I was challenged by them in a new and intense way.

In facing pain, I found it extraordinarily helpful that Jesus had himself undergone suffering. The Bible makes it plain that Jesus had to die for our sins, something I want to discuss later. I suppose it is possible that to pay the ransom for us Jesus could just have died swiftly, painlessly and easily. Instead of that, however, he underwent a death that involved terrible and profound agony. In the hours before his death, Jesus had undergone suffering at its deepest level in wave after wave of brutal trauma. There had been the moment in the Garden of Gethsemane, when Jesus had clearly seen in stark, graphic reality what he was going to have to go through. Mark's account states that there 'he took Peter, James and John along with him, and he began to be deeply distressed and troubled. "My soul is overwhelmed with sorrow to the point of death," he said to them' (Mark 14:33–34).

This period of intense psychological suffering was followed by a different sort of pain, as Judas kissed Jesus in the moment of betrayal to the Jewish leadership. He then underwent a succession of cruel interrogations with false allegations in front of the religious and civil authorities before being sentenced to death. He was flogged brutally by the soldiers, who thrust a woven crown of thorns on his head, repeatedly striking him with a staff as they mocked and spat at him. Then, after the agony of trying to carry his cross to the execution site, Jesus had nails hammered into his hands and feet before the cross was raised into a vertical position. Over the next three hours his life ebbed from him in an agony of thirst, pain and mental and spiritual torment that we cannot fully comprehend. Finally, after declaring, 'It is finished!' and committing himself to his Father, he bowed his head and died.

I found a great comfort in the fact that Jesus suffered and died not just a death, but one that was terrible and agonizing. He knew what pain was like then, and now, in heaven, he knows what it is like today. This is very helpful, as the reality is that for many people death does not occur suddenly and quietly in their sleep but often after months, or even years, of agony and pain. Yet for such people Jesus can be a tremendous help.

David Harding's story is a case in point. David was, for a long time, a man well known in Chorleywood. A chronic alcoholic, he was usually to be seen on summer evenings slumped on a bench in the middle of the village with a bottle by his side. Now 50, he had been addicted since the age of 20. He was invited to attend an Alpha course that our church was hosting but would often arrive in a drunken state. As far as the course was concerned, he viewed it as purely an academic exercise, although he was aware that those leading it actually seemed to believe what they taught. Nevertheless, he started to make friends with church people and began to feel that his life was turning around. On Boxing Day 1997, David decided to stop drinking. Within a few days he was experiencing chronic delirium tremens, the dreaded DTs of alcohol withdrawal. In this state, he saw demons and became aware that if he died he would go straight to hell. Terrorstruck, he felt that there was nothing stopping him from sinking into that awful pit. In desperation, David called out for Jesus to come and help him, asking him to take away his desire for alcohol. Immediately, the desire to drink was lifted from him and never returned. A few months later, however, the new David started to feel acute pain in his side. He was admitted to hospital, where he was diagnosed as having advanced cancer of the liver and told that he probably had only six months to live. David told his newly found Lord that he did not want to die, but that if it were to be so, he just wanted to thank him for the wonderful ten months that his new-found relationship had given him.

From then on David started to walk an uncharted journey with God. At each new and painful step, he felt that Jesus understood him completely because he too had walked the way of suffering to death. Jesus was an inspiration to David in his pains, but he was more than that, as David found that Jesus was present with him in the suffering. There were goodbyes, the pain, the humiliation of a decaying body, and ultimately David Harding died. David's testimony, given in church shortly before his death, was deeply moving. Despite his deterioration, his inner healing allowed it to be a message of triumphal joy.

Lying inert on my bed in hospital with an uncertain future I thought too not just about suffering, but also about death. The fact that Jesus suffered with us is an encouragement to all who go through pain. But the gospel story does not, of course, end with suffering and death. Death does not have the last word; resurrection does. David Harding's testimony was more than a statement that Jesus had been a comfort to him in his sufferings. It was an expression of confident hope that, in Jesus, death had been overcome.

There in my hospital ward I wondered where I would have been if my cry for help to Jesus had not been heard. I was certain that I would have been with him, but what, I wondered, would death have been like? Where, I asked myself, would I be now and what would I be doing? As I lay there, I went over in my mind some of the strange attitudes that we have to death in our modern culture.

I first really thought about death when I was 15. Tony Marsh was a keen sportsman and in my memory I see him vividly, literally flying through the air to catch a cricket ball being hit deep into the covers by a batsman from Wanganui Collegiate School in an annual school match. One day Tony was driving the tractor on his parents' sheep farm and it rolled over on him. Death was instantaneous. Suddenly Tony, so alive at the cricket match and only my age, was dead. Tony's funeral will for ever be etched on my memory. When I arrived, I found that the small wooden church was packed and I had to stand in the crowd that stretched from the church door down to the road. The service was relayed to us through speakers set up in trees. When the coffin was finally carried out, a long heavy silence, broken only by the sounds of sobbing from mourners, seemed to descend on us. I wanted to cry but somehow held my tears back; 15-year-old boys believe it is wrong to weep.

Then, shortly after Tony's funeral, it suddenly dawned on me that one day in the future, on some particular, real, definite day, I too was going to die. Until that moment I had always thought that death was what occurred to people when they grew old and that it happened to other people. I now realized that I was not exempt. At times, this appalling truth would overwhelm me as I recognized that my inevitable and inescapable death was a matter beyond my control. Somehow, a terrible, haunting fear seemed to have been unearthed in me. Since then, I have often wondered whether this abnormal fear of death had its roots in some traumatic birth experience. But whatever its origins, it was a problem that I had no answer to. Fear and confusion clouded my own views of death.

I now see that, to a greater or lesser extent, my own fear is widespread in our secular culture, although the ways in which it is handled vary from person to person. In general, we prefer not to discuss death at all. Even people in the medical profession, who frequently encounter death, may feel uncomfortable about it. Perhaps they feel a sense of failure when someone dies. Mary remembers a young doctor telling her of a surgeon who would never mention the word 'death' but described a person as having 'negative patient output'! This embarrassed reticence about death can lead to the bereaved feeling very isolated. They often recount how neighbours or friends will cross a road rather than talk to them in the street. If there is a conversation then it is often a stilted one, with the neighbour or friend making every attempt to avoid talking about the deceased. Ironically, the bereaved person longs to go over the events leading up to, and including, the death.

Sometimes people attempt to be philosophic or fatalistic about death. Increasingly we hear, in Elton John's words, of the deceased being compared to 'a candle in the wind'. The assumption seems to be that once the flame is extinguished, the life has gone for ever. There is nothing there about any future hope at all.

Many others are confused and unsure about any afterlife. In this confusion, strange theories emerge to bring comfort to the bereaved. They have little consistency and seem merely to provide a thin palliative hope that 'all will be well'. In some cases, the beliefs centre on some sort of idea about a survival of the personality. Maria Shriver, wife of Arnold Schwarzenegger, is a niece of President John Kennedy, and as someone related to that tragic family, she is familiar with death. She has recently published a best-selling children's book called *What's Heaven?* In it she quotes a response to a little boy's question arising from the death of his great-grandma: 'Great-Grandma's body is in a wooden box, but remember, her soul – all the things that made her a wonderful person – has already been taken to heaven by the angels.'

In other cases, these beliefs centre on 'being reunited with loved ones'. When Princess Diana died, the nation expressed a similar sort of belief in an afterlife. This was articulated in the popular press in such statements as 'Diana and Dodi are now united together in heaven'. Certainly the public seems to think that celebrities go to heaven. The definition of the 'loved ones' we will be reunited with is now very broad. Some years after the death of Eric Morecambe, his partner in comedy Ernie Wise died. At the news Des O'Connor joked, 'At last they are now together and knowing Eric he will say, "You're late again!"' Popular belief even has us being reunited with animals we have known. I have always enjoyed country and western music and many of the songs speak of the 'great ranch in the sky' where both the cowboys and their horses go. This of course raises numerous issues, as exemplified by the case of the small boy who, on being told that his granddad had 'gone to be with Ginger the cat', wailed that Granddad had hated the cat.

My own views on death were frankly no better until, in my 20s, I came to know Jesus Christ. What I found out then transformed my views on death for ever. My understanding of Jesus up until this time was fragmentary. It was as if I had been in a railway carriage, concentrating on reading a book, but every so often overhearing, from people on the seat behind, some snippet of conversation about someone. The knowledge I had about Jesus was similarly disconnected and the bits and pieces I knew made no overall sense at all.

All this confusion and incomprehension changed when

someone talked to me about Jesus Christ in a way that I could understand. The instantaneous burst of understanding and revelation that happened then was extraordinary. As I think of what happened, I am reminded of hearing Tracy Chapman in concert at the Royal Albert Hall. There, in that enormous hall, the lights went out and amid an expectant silence she walked onto the stage alone and sat down on a stool with her guitar. She played a chord and then sang in such a clear and powerful way that the words and meaning were perfectly clear and seemed to speak straight to me. I had a similar experience with Jesus. In this moment of understanding, I came to an abrupt realization that Jesus was God's answer to death and the future. All sorts of things became clear.

I understood that death was a disease that had infected the whole of humankind. I have seen the results of a deadly plague infecting a village in Africa; the disease had been brought into the village by one man but had then gradually spread throughout the entire village so that all died. This is a picture of what happened to humanity when sin entered the world through Adam. It not only caused his death but was also passed on to the rest of his race so that we too have come under the same sentence of death. Sin causes a fatal breakdown in our relationship with the God who sustains life; death is a direct consequence of sin.

In Mark's Gospel, we have the first biography of Jesus Christ and a third of the book is devoted to the circumstances surrounding the death of Jesus. Mark describes the significance of this event as a 'ransom', a concept that is very familiar to us. We often read in our newspapers of people who have been kidnapped and held by captors, only to be freed when money is paid. This image shows us one of the effects of Jesus' death; he gave his life in order that we might have ours back again and be freed from the bondage that our disobedience has caused. The Bible says, simply and profoundly, that Jesus 'died for our sins'.

Not only did Jesus die but he was also buried. We read in the Gospels how, after the body of Jesus was taken down from the cross, Joseph of Arimathea and Nicodemus carried it and buried it in a new stone tomb nearby. There can be no doubt that Jesus really did die. Some have fancifully suggested that he might have fainted or fallen into a coma from which he was resuscitated later in the cool of the tomb. Not only does this seem highly improbable, but if it was the case, then he could not have died for our sins and paid the penalty for our disobedience. But with Jesus buried in the grave, it must have seemed to his disciples as if death had triumphed.

They should have known better. During the three years before his death, Jesus had said to his disciples on a number of occasions that his life was going to end in Jerusalem. He told them that he would suffer, be rejected and killed and, after three days, would rise again. Apparently his words were never taken seriously, or properly understood, by the disciples, and his death came as a bewildering shock to them.

Yet the Gospels record that during his ministry Jesus demonstrated a mastery over death and on several occasions raised dead people to life. Luke 7 records how, when confronted by the funeral procession of the only son of a widow, Jesus addressed the corpse, 'Young man, I say to you get up.' The man sat up and began to talk. On another occasion, Jairus, the leader of a synagogue, approached Jesus and asked whether he would heal his dying daughter. By the time Jesus reached the house the girl had died. Refusing to be put off, Jesus went to her bed, took her body by the hand and said, '*Talitha koum*!' This is Aramaic and translates as, 'Little girl, I say to you, get up.' Here too the Gospels state that she immediately stood up and walked around.

In the record of the raising of Lazarus from the grave in John 11, we not only have an impressive account of Jesus' ability to overcome death but also some remarkable teaching on the subject. Lazarus of Bethany, the brother of Mary and Martha and a dear friend of Jesus, became very ill. Although Jesus was informed, he did not immediately make the journey to see him, but waited. When Jesus and the disciples finally arrived at Bethany, Lazarus was not only dead but had been buried in the tomb for four days. Jesus was met by the grief-stricken Martha who said to him, 'If you had been here, my brother would not have died. But I know that even now God will give you whatever you ask.' Martha was a committed follower of Jesus and must have seen his power to heal. Certainly she had faith that he could heal her brother. Even now, with Lazarus dead four days, she was confident that Jesus could ask God to intervene and bring him back to life. Jesus' response to her faith was to say, 'Your brother will rise again.' To this Martha replied, 'I know he will rise again in the resurrection at the last day.' In saying this, she was expressing the traditional belief of the Jewish religious party called the Pharisees. But Jesus proclaimed to her, 'I am the resurrection and the life. He who believes in me will live, even though he dies, and whoever lives and believes in me will never die. Do you believe this?' This statement is the pivotal statement of belief embraced by Christians worldwide, and confirms the gift of eternal life through faith in Jesus Christ. Martha's response to this was a strong one. 'Yes, Lord,' she said, 'I believe that you are the Christ, the Son of God, who was to come into the world.' In saying these words, Martha was making a deep statement of faith. The word 'Lord' is one that, as a Jewish believer, Martha would have used in her daily prayers to God, and here she was affirming her belief in the divinity of Jesus. In the word 'Christ' she was acknowledging him as the promised Jewish Messiah, the anointed servant of God to whom all their Scriptures pointed. In the phrase 'Son of God' she was expressing a belief that Jesus was the second person of the Trinity, God the Son.

Having recorded Jesus' claim of power to raise from the

dead, John's narrative moves to the tomb of Lazarus. Here Jesus ordered the stone removed from the entrance of the tomb. There were protests; after four days Lazarus was not simply dead but decomposing. Jesus, however, was undeterred and called out in a loud voice, 'Lazarus, come out!' At this summons, the dead man came out, wrapped in grave clothes, and Jesus said to those who were with him, 'Take off the grave clothes and let him go.'

There were probably other instances where Jesus brought people back to life that have not been recorded. Certainly Jesus sends his disciples to the imprisoned and despondent John the Baptist with, 'Go back and report to John what you hear and see: The blind receive sight, the lame walk, those who have leprosy are cured, the deaf hear, the dead are raised, and the good news is preached to the poor' (Matthew 11:4). Bringing the dead back to life was, it seems, a normal part of the ministry of Jesus.

The resurrection of Jesus that first Easter Sunday morning was the final and complete proof of his triumph over death. As he had raised others from the dead so now Jesus himself rose from the grave. Our greatest enemy had been destroyed!

As Christians we do not have to wait until we die before we can receive the good news of the resurrection. In fact, Scripture says that we receive eternal life as soon as we turn in faith to Jesus. As the Bible famously says in John 3:16, 'God so loved the world . . . that whosoever believes in him shall not perish but have eternal life.' Later in the same chapter, we read that 'whoever believes in the Son has eternal life'. It is a possession from the moment of our believing in Jesus.

The proof of this eternal life is the presence of the Holy Spirit, who comes to dwell in our hearts when we turn to Jesus. The Holy Spirit is an assurance of our future resurrection. Paul affirms this in Ephesians 1:13–14: 'Having believed, you were marked in him with a seal, the promised Holy Spirit, who is a deposit guaranteeing our inheritance until the redemption of those who are God's possession.' As I think of this, I am reminded of a time when I worked for Dalgety's in New Zealand and would sometimes go to the wool sale. In the warehouse would be hundreds of bales of wool, each one representing the wool from a whole flock of sheep. Buyers from around the world would gather for the sale and buy consignments of wool, but they would take just one bale. The understanding was that all the others would eventually follow. Jesus' resurrection is the guarantee that, in time, our own resurrections will follow.

When I became a Christian, my intellectual problems were answered. I now knew that Jesus had triumphed over death. Yet despite this knowledge, the thought of dying and being dead still scared me. This fear of death turned out to be a problem that I was to wrestle with for many years after becoming a follower of Jesus. I knew it was irrational, but I found that at times it would overwhelm me. I suppressed this fear for many years, but once I was ordained as a minister I found that I was regularly being confronted by the presence of death. Often, when visiting the bereaved or accompanying them to see a dead relative, I would find myself shaking and sweating profusely with fear.

I often heard preachers proclaim from 1 John 4 that 'God is love' and that 'perfect love casts out fear'. I had tried to accept this truth and to make it real in my life, but without success. The answer to my problem came at a meeting where Arthur Wallis was speaking. Arthur, whose book on revival, *In the Day of Thy Power*, is a classic, was a pioneer in the area of understanding the Holy Spirit. Through teaching and preaching, he sought to put his hearers in direct contact with the power of the Spirit. At this particular meeting, he was speaking on the power of God's love to drive out all fear. At the conclusion of the talk, he invited any who were struggling with fear in their lives to come up for prayer. I went up immediately and asked him to pray for me. As he prayed over me in Jesus' name, I felt a surge of something leaving from deep within my heart and it was replaced by a peace that has never left me. My fear of death had gone for ever; I had learned that the risen Jesus is able to deal with the fear of death that can grip our hearts.

The author of the letter to the Hebrews writes in chapter 2 about this experience that God's children have. 'He [Jesus] too shared in their humanity so that by his death he might destroy him who holds the power of death – that is, the devil – and free those who all their lives were held in slavery by their fear of death.'

As we consider the moment of our own death, it would seem that there are two things that we have to hold together. The first is that, for the believer, death will be like going to sleep. Jesus said to his disciples in John 11, 'Lazarus has fallen asleep but I am going to wake him up.' Elsewhere, when commenting on the condition of Jairus' daughter, Jesus said that she was not dead but asleep. I believe that Jesus will awaken us from that sleep. The second truth, which we need to hold in tension with the first, is that awaking in the presence of Jesus will be an immediate experience. Jesus, it is reported, was crucified between two thieves. Luke 23:39–43 gives the details. The first thief was very cynical and challenged Jesus to demonstrate he was the Messiah by miraculously getting off the cross. The other, however, saw the truth of the situation and acknowledged that while he and his comrade were guilty and merited punishment, Jesus was innocent. With his life ebbing from him, the second thief said, 'Jesus, remember me when you come into your kingdom.' From the broken figure on the central cross came the wonderful answer, 'I tell you the truth, today you will be with me in paradise.'

The apostle Paul echoes this truth when he writes to

fellow Christians in the Greek city of Philippi and speaks of his 'desire to depart and be with Christ' (Philippians 1:23). He was enjoying the company of the Christian community and had a 'fruitful labour' serving the church, but he felt he would rather leave them and be with Jesus. He repeats this sentiment to those who followed Jesus in Corinth, writing in 2 Corinthians 5:8 that he 'would prefer to be away from the body and at home with the Lord'.

The teaching of Scripture is that the first event after our death is that of judgement. Hebrews 9:27 states that '. . . man is destined to die once, and after that to face judgment'. This judgement is based upon our decision concerning Jesus; if we have rejected him during our lifetime then we will not be with him after our death. God will be sealing the decision we have already made. However, for those of us who are believers in Christ, the Scriptures reveal that God has planned an incredible future for us, including the momentous privilege of being with Jesus Christ when he returns to earth.

Thinking back now on my experiences, I feel that I have already undergone a rehearsal for death. Thrown about like a piece of rag in the wave at Himatangi Beach I had every reason to believe that I was about to die. I felt my neck breaking, knew the excruciating pain racing out through my neck, arms and back, had my chest squashed and was unable to breathe. At that moment, on the very edge of the darkness of unconsciousness, just as I thought I was about to die, I prayed, 'Jesus, help me!'

In retrospect, I realize that everything I had believed about Jesus and his power to raise from the dead came into play at that point of supreme crisis. In that moment, I realized that I had confidence that, even if death were to take me, Christ would be with me and would raise me in due course. Maybe my experience there, in a tiny way, reflects that of Job who, in the midst of his own appalling sufferings, was able to say with confidence: 'I know that my Redeemer lives, and that in the end he will stand upon the earth. And after my skin has been destroyed, yet in my flesh I will see God; I myself will see him with my own eyes – I, and not another. How my heart yearns within me!' (Job 19:25–27).

9
Waves of the Spirit

Waves have always fascinated me. I have sat on rocks above beaches all over the world, doing nothing but watching and listening to the incoming surf. I find myself captivated by the huge variety of waves. At one end of the scale are the mild, rolling surges that scamper gently up and across smooth shining sands; at the other are the violent crashing explosions of energy, as mighty breakers hit protruding rocks, throwing cascades of water high into the air.

As a surfer, I have come to know waves better than most. One well-known feature is that strong breaking waves usually come in sets. Once one wave has broken, maybe five or six more will follow before the sea calms for a while. This quiet period – the lull – is where the waves build up before another cycle of breakers. In the lull, there are usually a number of gentle swells, each of which is stronger than the previous one. Finally, the waves start to break again.

As I lay on my bed recovering in New Zealand, where great waves so often lash the coastlines, I would often think about the sea and the waves. In addition to reliving that terrible moment when the waves had struck me, and experiencing again the pain as my neck broke, I also found myself contemplating the whole nature of waves. The word 'parable' means 'to put things side by side'; what you see in the natural world reflects, or parallels, what you cannot see in the spiritual world. I felt that waves, with their patterns of lulls, building swells and then sequences of breakers, were a parable of what I have known of the visitations of the Holy Spirit during the last 30 years.

One thing I have learned is that prior to his coming in power in a new way, the Holy Spirit first creates what can be called a godly dissatisfaction. I find this rather like the lull in between the sequences of breakers. I first experienced this in the mid-1960s when I was a theological student at London College of Divinity, Northwood, Middlesex. My religious practice had become a formality. I seemed to be going through a process of saying a liturgy, singing uninspiring hymns, reading a Bible that lacked any life and saying dry, formal prayers. The truth that I could be in a life-changing relationship with Jesus Christ completely eluded me. In my more thoughtful moments my frustration was such that I sometimes used to say aloud, 'There must be more than this!' Coupled with this growing belief that there must be more was an experience of such spiritual dryness and barrenness that I felt desperate. I went through the usual Christian disciplines, but they simply made me feel self-righteous but dead. I was doing what was expected of a committed Christian, but it was all on the outside. The verdict delivered by the risen Christ on the church in Laodicea in Revelation 3:17 seemed to ring in my ears: 'You say, "I am rich; I have acquired wealth and do not need a thing." But you do not realise that you are wretched, pitiful, poor, blind and naked.' The only difference – and it was little comfort – was that I had become aware of the gulf between what I was and what I pretended to be. Yet in this personal spiritual desert, there came a desire to pray and seek the face of God. And, at the same time, I started to meet many other people also going through the same experience. I recognized that God was leading us all into a desert in order that we could seek him desperately. What could we expect from him? We knew that the key to our problems was surely the ministry of the Holy Spirit.

As a theological student, I knew about the Holy Spirit intellectually. I knew about the outpouring of the Holy Spirit on the infant church on the day of Pentecost that is recorded in Acts 2, and I often thought of it as a prototype for future visitations by God.

I also knew the Old Testament background to this outpouring. There, the Holy Spirit had fallen upon and filled particular individuals to equip them for special tasks. For the most part these were men and women who had leadership roles in Israel and they included kings like David, on whom 'the Spirit of the LORD came in power' after Samuel the prophet had anointed him with oil (1 Samuel 16:13). They also included prophets like Micah, who said confidently, 'But as for me, I am filled with power, with the Spirit of the LORD' (Micah 3:8), and judges, or leaders, like Gideon, of whom it was recorded, 'Then the Spirit of the LORD came upon Gideon' (Judges 6:34). Yet I also knew that in the Old Testament the prophets looked forward to a wider giving of the Spirit in the future. A key passage there was Joel chapter 2, where we read a wonderful prophecy of the Spirit's coming: 'And afterwards, I will pour out my Spirit on all people. Your sons and daughters will prophesy, your old men will dream dreams, your young men will see visions. Even on my servants, both men and women, I will pour out my Spirit in those days.' The prophet Joel here indicates that the Spirit will be given to far more than the selected few. Furthermore, manifestations of the Spirit would be seen especially among young people who will prophesy, young men who will see visions and the elderly who will 'dream dreams'. On that first day of Pentecost Peter had taken this text, with its promise of a comprehensive and all-inclusive outpouring of the Spirit, as being fulfilled on that day. The implication to me was that the power of the Spirit ought to be available for us in the church today.

I also knew that in the Old Testament the coming of the Spirit was associated with the refreshment and blessing of God's people. Another Old Testament prophecy about the pouring out of the Spirit helped here. In Isaiah 44:2–3, the Lord speaks through Isaiah to his people: 'Do not be afraid, O Jacob, my servant, Jeshurun, whom I have chosen. For I will pour water on the thirsty land, and streams on the dry ground; I will pour out my Spirit on your offspring, and my blessing on your descendants.' Not only did Isaiah too see that the Spirit would one day be more widely poured out than he ever had been before, but that this would be as welcome as water poured out on a dry, arid desert land. The recipients of the Spirit then would be thirsty and longing for his coming. Jesus must have had this in mind when, at the Feast of Tabernacles, he spoke to the crowd with a loud voice, 'If anyone is thirsty, let him come to me and drink. Whoever believes in me, as the Scripture has said, streams of living water will flow from within him' (John 7:37). This reviving power of the Spirit was what I wanted.

But how did we get the Spirit to come upon us today? Here I was helped by knowing that in the Old Testament the coming of the Spirit in power was associated with prayer and repentance. After the dedication of the temple by Solomon, Scripture records in 2 Chronicles 5:13–14 that 'the temple of the LORD was filled with a cloud, and the priests could not perform their service because of the cloud, for the glory of the LORD filled the temple of God'. Solomon then makes one of the most powerful prayers in Scripture and asks that the temple would be a place where God would meet all the needs of his people, and at the end of the petition, fire falls from heaven and consumes the sacrifices. The

Lord then appears to Solomon at night and gives him a promise regarding future days when the people of God would fall into rebellion and experience the divine judgement: 'If my people, who are called by my name, will humble themselves and pray and seek my face and turn from their wicked ways, then will I hear from heaven and will forgive their sin and will heal their land' (2 Chronicles 7:14). This principle I believe still stands, and days of praying and waiting for the Holy Spirit become days of heart-searching and times of repentance. On the first day of Pentecost 120 followers of Jesus had gathered to pray, as was their habit (Acts 1:14), and to wait 'for the promise of the Father' as he had commanded them.

I also knew from church history that there had been many subsequent outpourings of the Spirit, whether they had been termed 'revivals' or 'awakenings'. They too had fallen on many people, had refreshed the spiritually thirsty and had been similarly birthed in prayer and repentance. Perhaps curiously to us today, the last recent example of such a working of God was not one that we looked to very much then. The Azusa Street, Los Angeles, revival in the first decade of the twentieth century had not affected the mainstream churches but had instead given rise to a new denomination, the Pentecostals. In many places they were still suspect. In fact I remember seeing on the noticeboard of an old Anglican church an advertisement for a series on religious cults which included the Pentecostals! Nevertheless, along with others, I found myself with a craving for a new, fresh working of the Holy Spirit.

It was with many of these thoughts and expectations that Mary and I joined regularly with others at Northwood who also longed for another Pentecost, to pray for a visitation of God's Spirit. During this time of waiting and seeking, we were introduced to a group that met with John and Gay Perry in their vicarage at St Andrew's Church in Chorleywood.

This gathering for prayer commenced at ten at night and often went on into the early hours of the morning. Sometimes the Holy Spirit would touch those present and this would result in times of great laughter and joy. However, we knew that these moments were not the outpouring that we all prayed and longed for. As we met in this way we soon discovered that everywhere we went others were also gathering to pray and wait upon the Lord. We also attended regularly a night of prayer for revival that was held at various locations within the city of London. Expectation was growing. We were in a 'lull', but the swells were growing in strength and we believed that this movement of God would soon turn into a breaking wave.

The Holy Spirit's nature is such that he never comes when, where or how we expect. He is like the wind, which blows when and how it wills and never issues a weather forecast. When it did break, the wave surprised many people. Soon becoming known as the Charismatic Wave, it mainly affected the historic churches and stayed within them; no new denominations were founded. In this respect it was very different from the first or Pentecostal Wave.

Paul was used by God to bring a charismatic wave of the Spirit to the church in Ephesus. The event Luke describes in Acts 19 happened around a quarter of a century after the first wave of the Holy Spirit that happened at Pentecost. When Paul layed his hands on and prayed for the 'about twelve' followers of Jesus there, it is recorded that 'the Holy Spirit came on them, and they spoke in tongues and prophesied'.

What happened at St Andrew's in the 1960s reflected what many churches worldwide were starting to experience. The Holy Spirit fell sovereignly and spontaneously on those who had been gathering to pray. One of the main features of this outpouring of the Spirit was that the majority who experienced it spoke in tongues.

As with natural waves, a wave of the Spirit is at its most

powerful at the moment of breaking. I believe it is important that, at such a point, we enter into what God is doing. As Shakespeare comments, 'There is a tide in the affairs of men which, taken in the flood, leads on to fortune.' As any surfer knows, to miss a wave is an irretrievable action. Equally, though, those who have ridden waves are also aware that to catch a powerful wave can be both exhilarating and hazardous. So it is when we let the Spirit lead either us or our churches.

The prophet Ezekiel saw vividly the implications of being prepared to submit and enter into the uncontrollable flow of God's Spirit. In a vision recorded in chapter 47, he saw water flowing out of the restored temple, presumably symbolizing the outpouring of God's life-giving Spirit. As he watched it an angelic being joined him and led him along the course of the river which was flowing into the Judean Desert and into the Dead Sea. After walking together for a quarter of a mile, the angel led Ezekiel through the river, which at this point was up to the prophet's ankles. After another quarter of a mile, the water was knee high; after another, it was waist deep. Finally, it had risen to a height that made it impossible to wade. The only way to cross it now was to swim.

During the 1970s I had a number of significant meetings with David Watson, who was Vicar of St Michael's, York, and a major leader in the Charismatic Wave of the Spirit, and whose early death was a sad loss to the church. We had first met when I was researching for my book, *Springtime in the Church*, and David had made a number of noteworthy visits to St Andrew's. They included one memorable evening service when, at the conclusion of his sermon, over a hundred people became followers of Jesus. Over lunch one day, he asked me a very perceptive question. Did I think that the present springtime in the church created by the Charismatic Wave would lead into a summer followed by a spiritual harvest? Or would the spring be aborted and lead into a winter?

Certainly there were remarkable fruits: in quantitative terms David Barrett, the church historian, estimated that worldwide over 120 million people were affected by this wave of the Spirit. I have described some of the less easily measurable effects of the Charismatic Wave in the earlier chapters of this book. Nevertheless, it did not reach its full potential. God's intended springtime was aborted primarily, I believe, through lack of spiritual leadership. The missing dimension was the gathering into the church of those who had not heard of a living Jesus and his love for them. I believe that this should have been a major outworking of that wave. It was not.

The weaknesses in leadership were, with hindsight, evident early on. The percentage of vicars and pastors involved was relatively small in proportion to the numbers of lay people involved. There were phrases, some tactful, some not, used by the lay people to describe the majority of leaders who kept back from involvement. They were 'open', or 'waiting upon God to see the fruits', or more simply – and more bluntly – 'sitting on the fence'. With such a leadership, no initiative in the world, whether in business, industry or the church, could make an impact.

This was confirmed to me in a vision that I had as this wave was breaking on the churches. In my vision, I was on a hill and looking into the distance. Below me, a road ran from left to right, and between me and the road was a field of wheat. Then I saw that beyond the road lay another wheat field that stretched to the horizon. Then this image faded and I saw a sphere spinning above me. As I watched, countries appeared on it and then suddenly they all became fields of wheat. Two scriptures came into my mind. The first was words spoken to the disciples by Jesus prior to Pentecost in Acts 1:8: 'You will receive power when the Holy Spirit comes on you; and you will be my witnesses in Jerusalem, and in all Judea and Samaria, and to the ends of the earth.' Each of these areas fitted into the three sections of the vision. The second scripture came from a conversation Jesus had with his disciples in Samaria after the woman at the well had become a disciple: 'Do you not say, "Four months more and then the harvest"? I tell you, open your eyes and look at the fields! They are ripe for harvest' (John 4:35).

As the 1970s ended, disturbing articles appeared in Christian newspapers and magazines that questioned the validity of the Charismatic Wave. The impression they gave was that it had simply petered out. I believe that this was a misunderstanding of what had happened. In the nature of things, waves eventually run out of momentum and then, having run their course, they ebb away. In such a lull, however, a stronger wave may be starting to build up.

During the period of this lull, I found myself badly affected. Again I had the feelings of godly dissatisfaction and a sense of spiritual dryness and questioning. Again I found that I had slipped into a religious routine; this time though it was based on the 'charismatic' traditions that had been formulated over more than a decade. Now we had a 'spontaneous' liturgy, but we had somehow acquired regular, appointed times when we were open to receive words or revelations from God. New hymns or songs had replaced many of the ancient hymns, but they no longer created life in the heart; the sick were being regularly prayed for, but with little or no effect. Again I found myself saying, 'There must be more than this!' It was a dry time and I found myself with an uncanny sense of *déjà vu*. I had been here before.

Now, though, I was involved in leading a church – a hard process without life in your heart. I found it difficult to help others, many of whom were experiencing what I was. In addition to my church responsibilities, I was also leading the Faith Sharing Ministry, with its vision to take what we were learning as a church to other churches. But as we travelled, I felt like a man with empty pockets.

In the Eastern church it is common to have a *poustinia* – a place of spiritual retreat where one can contemplate and pray. I had discovered that the Grail community in Pinner, a lay Roman Catholic body based on prayer and service, had many *poustinias* situated in the woods or gardens. Each one had a bed, table and chair, and they had been used since 1974. Now, like some wounded animal, I sought solitude there. Once a week, if I was not travelling, I would try and retreat to my *poustinia,* known as The Priory Hut, and spend time waiting upon God and seeking him for his presence.

Early one evening in 1980, I was driving across London to speak at a meeting south of the Thames. I had chosen to go through Chelsea and over the Vauxhall Bridge, but there was a great deal of traffic and for long periods everything settled into total gridlock. I was stopped in a main street when I heard an inner, audible voice say, 'I am relocating the centre of renewal from California to London. A third wave is coming.'

I had already heard rumours concerning John Wimber, Pastor of the Vineyard Church in Yor Belinda, California. From this church he had started, mainly with young people, others had been planted in various American cities. It seemed that there was a powerful work of the Holy Spirit flowing through these young churches, manifested in the creation of new songs and styles of worship. It was reported that those who led the worship had had an anointing of the Holy Spirit in a way that enabled them to bring their congregations into the presence of God. I had also heard that through revelations that the Holy Spirit inspired, the believers were able to bring God's healing power to the sick and suffering. Finally, in 1981, John Wimber and a team of young people came to St Andrew's, with the dramatic results I described previously.

This powerful wave of the Spirit that swept over many of the churches in the 1980s came to be known worldwide as the Third Wave. Its main ministry seems to have been to equip God's people to minister the life of Jesus to others, and in it the Spirit was poured out, giving revelations concerning the causes of people's physical, psychological or spiritual conditions. Another area of importance in this Third Wave was in the equipping of people for ministry. Paul wrote to the Christians in Ephesus concerning this process, making the point in Ephesians 2 that when Jesus ascended to heaven he gave gifts, enabling believers to be apostles, prophets, evangelists, pastors or teachers. The implication is that those so gifted were to train others whom the Lord had called. In this new wave of the Spirit's work that occurred in the 1980s many people were gifted and anointed in this way in their ministries. Barrett has estimated that some 20 million people were affected by this wave of the Spirit.

However, this wave ebbed too. By the late 1980s a number of us were in a lull for the third time in our Christian lives. It was another *déjà vu* situation.

In the summer of 1993 I was invited by Bishop David Pytches to speak at the final night of the New Wine conference. I again climbed the hill above the farm where we lived for the week and sat taking in the beauty all around me. Behind, rising in the far distance, was the ruined church on the hill overlooking Glastonbury. Below me was a field of corn that stretched down the lower hillside to a stream, beyond which cows grazed in front of the old farmhouse and cottages where we stayed. Overhead the clouds were racing across the sky and a breeze was blowing into my face. In my heart I was quietly seeking a word for the evening meeting. Suddenly I found myself being engulfed in an experience of the Holy Spirit that somehow touched all my senses. I can best describe the vision by simply quoting the description of it that I gave in my sermon.

I heard the sound of many waters,
I saw many waters, waterfalls
plunging into deep valleys.
Waterfalls, dropping gently by stages.
I saw wide rapids,
water was shallow and dancing in the light.
It was a picture of fun and laughter.
I saw other rapids,
racing down a deep gorge and
throwing up billows of spray.
I saw a river,
slow, powerful and majestic.
I saw rivers,
gushing down mountains,
meandering through water meadows.
I saw streams in valleys,
and creeks in forests.
I saw springs,
bubbling and gushing up.
I saw rains,
falling upon the earth;
some fell softly like mist,
others fell in torrents.
I heard the sound of many waters,
then I heard the voice of God say,
'I am coming in many ways to
refresh my people.'

Five months later, on the 20th January 1994, the wave of blessing that I had foreseen broke in the congregation of the Airport Vineyard in Toronto, Canada, and spread out rapidly to the world. This was an outpouring of the Spirit that could apparently be transmitted through prayer and the laying on of hands to others. With thousands of others from all parts of the world, I visited the church. At every meeting, the Holy

Spirit came in gusts and sometimes I found myself shaking almost uncontrollably. In retrospect, I feel that he was shaking things from my life that had previously bound me.

There was more, however, as I found out one afternoon, when I attended a meeting for church leaders. As we waited upon God, the Holy Spirit took me and literally hurled me across the room with a power so great that I was unable to resist it in any way. It felt like being caught up in a whirlwind or hurricane. I ended up on my back on the floor and gave out the loudest roar or shout I have ever heard. Whatever happened on that particular day and during that week certainly changed my effectiveness as a minister of the gospel, and I found that the Holy Spirit seemed to come in greater power in response to what I said. I found that this was also the case in the lives and ministries of all the other leaders I knew who had gone to Toronto. Was the Toronto Blessing a further wave of the Spirit? I believe it *was* a wave, but not in the sense the others were. In the world of sea waves, sometimes within the lulls of the cycles of large waves you get small surges of water in the wake of waves that have just gone. Whatever the Toronto Blessing was, it was not the big Fourth Wave that I believe is still to come.

These waves of the Spirit's outpouring that I have described seem to have made an impact on churches in many positive ways. Whenever the Holy Spirit acts, Jesus Christ becomes the focus of those involved with the Spirit. Religion, with all its traditions and trappings, is replaced by a relationship with Jesus, and to those entering into it this becomes life-changing.

The new life that the Spirit brings is expressed in many new forms of worship. Recently, within a period of three weeks, I have been speaking at conferences in Germany, Ireland, Holland, Finland, Lapland, Stoke-on-Trent, Ashford and Basingstoke. The one thing all these conferences had in common was new songs of worship. These had been written by those whom the Holy Spirit was touching and as an expression of their new-found love for Jesus and their joy in believing. Many congregations that have been visited by the Spirit are now characterized by biblical teaching and a developed prophetic and healing ministry. They have grown and planted churches and taken initiatives in caring for the poor.

One issue though is striking. These waves of the Spirit that have come upon the church since the 1960s have not been associated with large numbers of conversions. Church numbers have mainly increased because people have transferred from 'dead' churches to those where the Holy Spirit has been welcomed. An exception to this has been where the Alpha course has brought outsiders into a living faith in Christ.

Now I believe that there is another wave beginning to build and I sense that this will be known as the 'Harvest Wave'. Except for the Pentecostal Wave at the beginning of the last century, these waves have only really had an effect on churches, and have had little influence at community or national level.

I believe this next wave, the Harvest Wave, will be different.

10
In the Pipe

Over the last 30 years I believe God has been at work within his church through these various outpourings of the Spirit. In the Charismatic Wave, I believe the Holy Spirit was teaching the church to minister his gifts. The Third Wave introduced the churches to the power of God and the ministry of the Holy Spirit and, finally, the Toronto Blessing not only refreshed the church but introduced it to the unpredictability of the Spirit. Yet despite these works, there have been things that have remained stubbornly unchanged and unaffected by them all. It is my belief that in preparation for this next great wave, God is about to deal with those things that have resisted all that he has been doing so far.

One reason for my confidence is a striking dream that I had. In it, I found myself standing in the middle of an ancient church building. There were objects buried just below the surface of the floor and I began to dig them up. As I did, I was aware of someone I knew, who was a keen traditionalist on church matters, sitting nearby and watching me. As I dug I found a gold case and looked at it. The hinge had broken and it seemed as if at some time in the past someone had tried unsuccessfully to mend it. On it, I could make out the date, '1937'.

Now somehow I started to take up the floorboards of the church. These were complicated, with the boards crossed as if there were two sets, one running diagonally and the other laterally. At first, I found dozens of golden musical instruments, then as I lifted the lateral boards I discovered beneath them an incredible ship. It seemed to be the largest ship I had ever seen and as I started digging it up, I realized that other people were now helping me. As great areas of the deck were uncovered, I became aware that the ship's engine was thudding. In one part of the great ship, I saw an area that I felt we might live in. It needed much renovation, but I was certain that it could be done. Beneath me, the engines roared into life and the ship started to move. But the mud held it fast, and straining to be free of the mud the vessel continued to surge backwards and forwards. I knew somehow that in time it would be free. In my dream now I saw an evangelist friend of mine appear and together we walked to the bow, where we stood looking back down the deck. I saw that the ship was an enormous grain carrier with large holds that had been cleansed ready for the harvest. I realized that its destination was the harvest fields of the world.

For many days after this unforgettable dream, I pondered on what I had so vividly observed. Slowly I pieced together an interpretation. It seemed to me that for many decades people had tried to mend traditional religion, but with no success. The discovery of the musical instruments symbolized the renewal of authentic Spirit-inspired worship. The grain ship itself was the church that the Lord was seeking to free from 'strongholds' and send to collect the harvest. But the church was stuck in the mud, although the engines were running.

I believe that the waves of the Spirit that have broken over the churches during the last 30 years were meant to thrust a renewed and invigorated church out into the community to share the love of Jesus. However, except in some exceptional situations, this has not happened. The reason is that there have been 'strongholds' within congregations that have never been addressed and which have held churches captive and untouched by the Spirit. As in my vision, they have been stuck in the mud.

The apostle Paul was familiar with the concept of strongholds within the church. To the church in Corinth he wrote: 'For though we live in the world, we do not wage war as the world does. The weapons we fight with are not the weapons of the world. On the contrary, they have divine power to demolish strongholds. We demolish arguments and every pretension that sets itself up against the knowledge of God, and we take captive every thought to make it obedient to Christ' (2 Corinthians 10:3–5).

The creation of strongholds in a congregation can take place very insidiously. I once visited a church where one particular man appeared to have more authority than the vicar. As a member of the choir, he was given the responsibility of keeping the gowns in good order and was given keys to a church cupboard where the robes were kept. This, however, was not enough and over many years he borrowed keys and had copies cut. Finally, he had acquired the keys to all the buildings and had assumed authority over the whole church complex. The matter was never challenged and consequently he had to be approached and his permission sought for access to any part of the church. If it were not such a serious matter it would be hilarious! The result was that he had become a stronghold against the congregation.

A stronghold in a church exerts a stubborn power, obstructing the work of the Holy Spirit and opposing the God-given authority that belongs to the authorized leader. The apostle Paul wrote that Christians are engaged in warfare with hostile spiritual forces and behind these strongholds are indeed spiritual powers. Such forces are especially able to exert their power and influence through a person who is not wholly submitted to Jesus Christ.

It is not just people, however, who can become strongholds in a church; inanimate objects can too. Such strongholds often lie dormant until the leader wants to rearrange things in the church so that a more relevant form of worship can be introduced. A common scenario is for plans to be announced for the removal of front pews that have dominated and cramped the sanctuary for many centuries so that there can be a large, carpeted stage. Such a new structure, it is argued, will allow the congregation excellent visibility, as well as providing a platform for the worship group and communion table. Yet I have known many churches where a powerful group have used the pews to create a stronghold over the leadership's plans. In one well-known church, this group took the leadership to a consistory court where a compromise decision had to be reached because the legal fees to proceed were beyond the budget of the vicar. It was extraordinary to see six ancient freestanding pews cluttering up the newly carpeted worship area.

Powerful strongholds in the church start with unbelief and cynicism. Although there is a strong spiritual focus in our culture, this is mainly of the New Age variety – that useful umbrella term for all forms of spiritual experience ranging from fortune-telling to white magic. Coupled with this is the growth of many religions including Buddhism, Hinduism and Islam. Against this background, vast sections of the church have lost their nerve and have been imprisoned in a stronghold of unbelief.

My response to these strongholds is to remind myself that the Christian faith is supernatural. It involves God supernaturally becoming a man in Jesus Christ. Jesus lived, died, was buried and rose again supernaturally from the dead. He went to heaven and sent the Holy Spirit not only to indwell those who believed in him, but also to work through them in power. Yet the Holy Spirit and his workings have become an embarrassment to many parts of the church. In many cases they have been rejected as being either due to irrational beliefs or a result of emotional instability. Some have even suggested that the demonic is involved. The result is that waves of the Spirit sent by God have largely been deflected by unbelief.

When I started the Faith Sharing Ministry in 1974, I discussed the setting up of the work with Robert Runcie, who was then the Bishop of St Albans. He was very encouraging and licensed me to minister outside my diocese. Each year he would invite me back to share with him what I had seen the Lord doing. On one occasion, we were discussing the ministry of our teams as it related to the church at large. He said that he saw the Faith Sharing Ministry as functioning on the circumference of the traditional church. Then, as an aside, he said that actually the circumference was the centre. I interpreted that to mean that life in the Spirit was predominantly exercised outside the centre, which remained motivated by tradition.

Lifeless traditions are strongholds that have resisted the waves of the Spirit. Such regular routine practices are safe and predictable, creating a form of religion in which there is no spiritual power. 'We don't do it that way,' is the plaintive cry of tradition. What results is the appearance of respectability but the absence of the Spirit's power. Our experience of God is so often restricted by our fear of change.

I believe that because there has been such resistance to the waves of the Spirit, there has been little power available for life-changing meetings with Jesus. This has led to strongholds of both a spiritual and immoral nature being established in congregations. Strongholds thrive on compromise that opposes truth.

One area where this has been tragically manifest is in the area of sexual morality. It is sadly not uncommon that during one of our team visits a leader's wife will confide that her husband is having an affair with a younger member of the church. In one extreme case, I ministered to a large congregation where a previous pastor who had been married had had sexual relationships with 16 women in the church. He left, but tragically his successor also ended up committing adultery and he in turn had to leave. The result was the resignation of the remaining leadership. This stronghold of immorality also led to an abnormal and oppressive control over the congregation so that they were unable to denounce what was happening and were forced to conform to a leadership that was saying one thing and doing another.

Strongholds can be created in other ways, with similar deadly results. I have known of members of Anglican churches who attend the Sunday celebration of the Lord's Supper and yet during the week attend seances or consult mediums or horoscopes to seek the future direction of their lives. Such spiritual adultery creates a stronghold within individual lives and congregations.

Oddly enough, the vicar or church leader may himself become a major stronghold against a congregation. Often the root of this is a deep insecurity within his life – sometimes the result of traumatic events within childhood. Whatever the cause, it shows itself in a craving to control everything and everyone within a church. In worship and other meetings, an extraordinary effort may be expended to make sure that nothing happens that is outside the leader's control.

I have flown over the Great Barrier Reef many times on my way to and from New Zealand. A vast coral reef stretching along the north-eastern coast of Australia, it protects the coastline from powerful waves from the Pacific Ocean. When these waves strike the reef, they are resisted and their energy is lost so that they become reduced to nothing. A pathetically similar picture can be seen in so many churches where various strongholds have become like such barrier reefs, reducing and resisting the waves of the Spirit.

If only! This was the tearful cry of Jesus when he came to Jerusalem for the final time and wept over the city, the very centre of worship for God's people. 'If you, even you, had only known on this day what would bring you peace – but now it is hidden from your eyes,' he said (Luke 19:42). The result of their rejection of God's initiative was the terrible destruction of Jerusalem and the temple within a generation, at the hands of the Roman army under Titus.

If only the church had responded fearlessly to the waves of renewal that have swept it during the last 30 years. What blessings we might have seen! The wave of paganism that threatens to overwhelm us would surely have been pushed back.

These regrets came to me forcefully once, when I spoke on the Omega TV programme in the Netherlands. That night the subject of the programme was 'There must be more to life than meets the eye'. One of the guests had been a practising witch, with a considerable degree of seniority in 'the craft'. The presenter asked him if, as a practising witch, he had known any spiritual power and if so what it could do. The ex-witch proceeded to tell how, besides having 'healing powers', he was able to see accurately into people's lives so that on a train journey he was able to look at his travelling companions and speak with discernment into their lives. The fascinating point was that he admitted to being unable to penetrate the lives of Christian people, who were protected from his power. Christians who were merely nominal though did not have the same protection. As he finished, the presenter brought me into the discussion by asking if there was any spiritual power in the church. He finished the question by saying, rather tragically, that not many people would associate the church with spiritual power. I responded by giving an illustration of God's power at work in the church in the healing of a friend.

Later, though, sobered by the interviewer's perception of a powerless church, I pondered on what would have happened to the church if it had allowed the Third Wave to flow without restriction. Would there now be a mature five-fold ministry, on the pattern of Ephesians 4:11, functioning in congregations? Would churches, equipped with God-anointed apostles, prophets, pastors, teachers and evangelists, have been functioning powerfully and effectively in their ministries? Surely, if that had happened, the values and practices of neo-paganism would certainly have been more successfully confronted, albeit at the cost of many martyrs. And the Fourth Wave would have surely made the members of God's church the happiest people on earth.

I believe that if the church had been more open to the Spirit's power, the following statement would have indeed been true: 'God's way of being human has been demonstrated in Jesus Christ, is available to all by the Spirit within and is currently being demonstrated in your local church.' At the moment the last part of this statement reads – rather sadly – like wishful thinking. I believe that this need not have been the case.

Since the coming of Jesus, it has been God's declared intention to reveal his Son to the nations through the church. In the twentieth century the church resisted three of God's major initiatives to cleanse, renew and empower it. I believe that, as a result, a mighty 'shaking' of judgement has already started in the house of God. We will be called to account.

The 17th October 1987 will always be a date I remember. I had risen early and was taking our cocker spaniel Ziggy for her regular walk up the nearby Chess Valley. This particular walk takes an hour and goes through farmland along a narrow country lane and back through a mature forest. As the forest came into view, I stopped dead, staring in absolute amazement and incredulity at what I could see. Of the entire forest, hardly one tree was standing. The rest were lying scattered around the hillside as if the contents of some gigantic box of matches had been tipped on the ground. The previous night a hurricane had struck the south coast and caused incredible devastation. The fact that Michael Fish, the TV weather presenter, had publicly denied a viewer's query about a pending hurricane passed into TV mythology.

As I stood taking in the situation I heard the inner audible voice of God say to me, 'I am about to shake the nations and the church.' Beginning the following month and continuing to this present time the whole of Europe was shaken apart. Political boundaries and regional spheres of authority that had been set up at the Yalta conference 40 years previously, fell down. Communism almost disappeared overnight. As with the hurricane, God swept across nations in a way that astonished onlookers. I believe that a similar shaking of the church has already started as God addresses not political boundaries but spiritual strongholds in his church.

This was confirmed to me by a most disturbing dream I had after the hurricane. It was in the same format as the awesome dreams and visions that the prophet Ezekiel had and tried to describe. What my dream actually indicated – the details are not relevant here – was indeed the judgements of God. As these judgements came, the church both misunderstood what was happening and misinterpreted the events, not only to itself, but also to the nation.

My belief is that in preparation for the Harvest Wave that will bring in the lost, God's judgement is being seen in the bringing down of strongholds. He is freeing his church in preparation for the outpouring of his Spirit and starting to deal with everything and everyone that is keeping his precious 'grain ship' trapped in the mud.

One of the major ways he is doing this is through the raising up of the prophetic ministry. This gifting is being released in a variety of ways. Whenever God is about to do something new, he tells his prophets and raises up his intercessors. There is a graphic account in the Acts of the Apostles (Acts 12:1–18) of how Peter was released from a physical prison that reflected a spiritual stronghold. King Herod Agrippa had lashed out at the church leadership in Jerusalem, having James beheaded and Peter imprisoned. Herod probably knew as much about Jesus as anyone else, but he was in rebellion against God. Through his hatred, a stronghold was placed upon Peter in the form of an imprisonment so thorough that 'four squads of four soldiers' guarded him around the clock. Paul writes in 2 Corinthians 10:4 that the church has weapons to demolish strongholds and the first weapon is prayer, and certainly it was employed here. We read (Acts 12:5) that while Peter was in prison the church gathered and was 'earnestly praying to God for him'. In answer to this serious intercessory prayer, the Lord dramatically broke the power of this stronghold. An angel appeared, Peter's chains fell off, and he was escorted to the freedom of a city street.

Today, as part of this progress, I believe that God is raising up his intercessors. Once, I was ministering to a young man who seemed to be severely demonized and a spiritual presence of evil held him powerfully. Praying in Jesus' name had produced some headway, but in the end we came to an impasse. Then one of our intercessors who, with others, had been praying for the situation said that she felt that God had shown her that the practice of Freemasonry within the family was the cause. When in prayer I placed the cross of Jesus between the young man and the generations of his family who had been involved in the Freemasons, the stronghold was broken and he was set free.

I have a pastor friend in the Netherlands called John Le Fir. The translation of his name, 'John the Fire', is an apt one for this elderly and godly man who comes from the former

Dutch colony of the Moluccas. Some years ago, in the Dutch city of Almelo, John started a church in the front room of his home. This started to grow, so new facilities were bought. However, the growth continued so that along with many other Moluccans up to 23 nationalities were meeting for worship on a Sunday. Eventually the growth reached a point where even larger facilities became necessary and this became something of a problem. Eventually a local school came on the market and the church applied to buy it. The school was perfectly suited for John's purposes. In pristine condition, it had a large hall, dining room, lounge and numerous well-appointed classrooms; there was so much space that a twelve-hundred-seat worship area looked possible. To the dismay of the church, the council refused their application to buy the building. Enquiries were made and it turned out that the main opposition to their having the building was the chairman of the council. It transpired that this man had said that he would not 'under any circumstances' allow the building to be bought by these people. The stronghold here was one of racism. Pastor John called the church to intercessory prayer and they met regularly, asking that the Lord would break the power of the stronghold. On one occasion, John asked that the Lord would send the chairman 'into the bush'. Within a week, he disappeared from the town for a month. When he returned he sold his house and moved away with his family. The church subsequently bought the school.

In the account of the early church in Acts 2:45 we read that many believers sold their property to give funds to the common purse. However, in Acts 5 we read that Ananias and Sapphira held back some money from their property sale while giving the impression that they had given everything. Here, plainly, was a stronghold of lies and dishonesty, and if this had been allowed to stand at the heart of the early church it would have been a real obstacle to others. The Holy

Spirit, however, revealed to Peter the true situation and he confronted it through a prophetic word. He said to Ananias, 'How is it that Satan has so filled your heart that you have lied to the Holy Spirit and have kept for yourself some of the money you received for the land?' (Acts 5:3). At this divine word, Ananias 'fell down and died'. A similar word to his wife produced a similar result, and she too died. Through this necessary action the power of this stronghold of lies that threatened the early church was broken.

What will this Harvest Wave be like? I sense it will have a number of characteristics. In preparation for its coming many strongholds will be brought down so that the wave, when it comes, can have its full effect. One of the most exhilarating, and addictive, experiences for the surfer is to ride his board through what is known in surfers' jargon as 'the pipe'. The pipe is formed when an enormous wave breaks over itself and briefly forms a long hollow under the breaker. In the pipe the surfer finds himself almost entirely surrounded by millions of tons of water. It is an exhilarating moment; all around is the greenish blue of the roaring sea, the power is immense and there is a feeling of absolute freedom. As the board under his feet cuts its way along the extending pipe, the surfer feels no strain or striving, but only the sensation of being carried along by an incredible and irresistible power.

I believe that when this Fourth Wave breaks it will be something like being in the pipe. The church will understand Jesus' words, 'You will receive power when the Holy Spirit comes upon you and you shall be my witnesses' (Acts 1:8). This new power will be manifested in the ways in which the Spirit will lead people into encounters with God. There will also be a powerful miraculous element, where even the chronically sick will be healed.

In this Fourth Wave, there will be a compulsion to tell others about Jesus and his love for them. My wife Mary has had two almost identical experiences in which God seemed to be saying to her, 'This is what it will be like when the wave breaks.' Once she was awoken early in the morning and was deeply filled by the Holy Spirit, and she felt waves of power flowing through her. Deep within she suddenly had an incredible compulsion to go and tell others about Jesus. So urgent was this compulsion that she found herself walking around the house and looking out of the windows for someone to tell. Unsurprisingly for half-past five on a winter's morning there were not many people about! In that experience, she felt the Lord was saying to her that although it was too early now, this was what it would be like when revival came.

Many other prophets have seen this Fourth Wave coming and some have made the mistake of naming the date and time. My dear friend John Wimber did this in 1991 when he called the church to a large conference at Wembley. A prophet he greatly respected and trusted had foretold that revival was coming to London, starting at that conference. But it was not to be. Subsequently others have also given dates.

However, when we study the prophets of Israel in the Bible we see that very rarely do they give dates, although there are exceptions: Jeremiah for example foretold the 70 years in exile; Isaiah (16:13) speaks of a prophecy being fulfilled within three years and, in 21:16, of a fulfilment within a year. More commonly the time of a prophecy is no more precisely given than in some phrase such as 'the days are coming'.

Two of our Faith Sharing Team leaders, Don and Noel Stocking, have a home in Salcombe, Devon. Built in 1904, it has been beautifully maintained. One evening Mary and I were in the antique pine furnished dining room, sitting at the table together praying. Behind me stood an old German grandfather clock with weights and a large disc pendulum.

The house had been empty for a number of months and the weights of the clock had dropped so that, this evening, it stood silent. In our prayers, Mary and I sought the Lord for what we believed would be the Harvest Wave of his Spirit. As we waited on the Lord, the clock suddenly started to tick loudly. Utterly amazed I looked around to see the pendulum now moving from side to side. The clock had commenced ticking at exactly 7.45. Mary looked at her watch, astonished to see that it too showed the time 7.45. 'The revival is coming,' she exclaimed, 'and it will come suddenly and on time.'

11
The Hidden Side of the Moon

Lying in the hospital bed in New Zealand I was confident at first that it would only be a matter of time before God would heal me completely. I was so certain of this that each time the consultant and his team visited, I was very positive, and if anything I exaggerated my well being to try and convince myself – and them – that a full healing was well underway. During these visits, they would test the strength and feeling in a hand by asking me to press my thumb and forefinger together or to push against one of their hands with my fingers. But week after week, my fingers stayed numb and dead. Slowly I began to realize that nothing was really happening and I asked Mr McCormick for a full prognosis of my situation. In his quiet, frank way, he told me that if my nerves had just been bruised then full sensation could return within a year, or two years at the most. However, if the nerves had been severed then there would be no return of feeling; not ever. After that, all too aware that feeling and life were not returning to some parts of my body, I began to review my whole attitude to healing. Could God heal me? Was it my lack of faith? How could a God of love and power *not* heal me? The questions mounted.

When I became a follower of Jesus Christ there was little

or no expectation among ordinary Christians that God could, or would, heal the sick. Healing in all its forms seemed to be entirely the province of the professionals: the trained medical doctors and psychiatrists. With the coming of the charismatic movement, all this changed and a fresh interest emerged in the healing ministry of the church. Before the charismatic rediscovery of the Holy Spirit, God was limited to working only in ways that our rational mind-sets, with their inbuilt prejudice against the supernatural, could understand. Faced with the evidence of a supernatural Christianity over the first hundred years of the church's history, the reaction was to say that such manifestations of the power of God had been limited to that period and, for some inscrutable reason, had then ceased. I had never found this argument convincing and in my heart I always believed that if God was all-loving and powerful then he would want to be involved for our good in our sicknesses as well as in every other aspect of our lives.

When John Perry arrived as Vicar at St Andrew's in 1966, he inherited a small nucleus of people who were praying for spiritual renewal. As they experienced what can only be described as a spontaneous outpouring of the Holy Spirit, they started a study of the early church in the Acts of the Apostles. In that book miracles occur regularly and this raised repeatedly the question as to whether similar sorts of things were to be expected today. Pursuing that question led back to the nature of the ministry of Jesus himself. After all, the early church seems to have been simply doing what it had been told to do.

According to Luke himself, the author of Acts, Jesus spelled out the manifesto for his ministry in his home synagogue of Nazareth. Standing up there, he unrolled the scroll of Isaiah given to him and read the following: 'The Spirit of the Lord is on me, because he has anointed me to preach good news to the poor. He has sent me to proclaim freedom for the prisoners and recovery of sight for the blind, to release the oppressed, to proclaim the year of the Lord's favour' (Luke 4:18–19; quoting Isaiah 61:1–2). Having read these words, Jesus announced to the assembled worshippers that this prophecy was fulfilled that very day in their hearing. The Gospels go on to record how, in many actions of healings and deliverance, Jesus demonstrated the fact that this ancient prophecy was indeed now fulfilled.

Jesus proclaimed the kingdom of God, a kingdom of spiritual power. As the rule of the kingdom came to bear on human conditions then men and women were healed. To those who were sick because they had disobeyed the will of God, Jesus spoke words of forgiveness. Where disobedience had resulted in a physical condition – as in the case of the paralysed man of Mark 2 or the man who sought healing at the Pool of Bethesda in John 5 – such words of forgiveness brought actual physical healing. Jesus was motivated in his healing by compassion towards the sick. In one of his summaries concerning the ministry of Jesus, Matthew writes that in addition to teaching and preaching the gospel, Jesus was 'healing every disease and sickness among the people. News about him spread all over Syria and people brought to him all who were ill with various diseases, those suffering severe pain, the demon-possessed, those having seizures, and the paralysed and he healed them' (Matthew 4:23–24). The three years of Jesus' ministry were characterized by healing in various forms and it seems plain that Jesus intended his followers to continue this ministry. During his ministry on earth he imparted to his disciples his authority and power so that they could do in his name what he had been doing. In Mark 6:7–12 we read that Jesus sent out the Twelve two by two, giving them authority over evil spirits. In verse 13 we are told that 'they drove out many demons and anointed many sick people and healed them'. Later Jesus sent out a group of 72 with a similar ministry. This enlarged group of disciples reported back to him with joy that 'even the demons submit to us in your name' (Luke 10:17). In the Great Commission that Jesus gave to all disciples in every age, recorded for us in Matthew 28, he says that we are to 'go and make disciples of all nations . . . and teaching them to obey everything I have commanded you'. In that command to teach and obey everything, healing must be included.

Certainly the book of Acts indicates that a similar multi-faceted ministry of teaching, preaching, healing and exorcism continued through the history of the early church. As the small praying nucleus at St Andrew's studied the life of the early church, they discovered that the key to all the supernatural activity was the Holy Spirit. This again brought them back to the Gospels and to the pattern of Jesus.

Before the start of his public ministry Jesus was baptized by John the Baptist. After being immersed in the River Jordan, Jesus prayed (Luke 3:21). As he was talking with his heavenly Father we read that the 'Holy Spirit descended on him in bodily form like a dove'. From then on the Gospels (and Luke in particular) recount how Jesus was 'full' of the Spirit and led by the Spirit (Luke 4:1); how he ministered in the 'power' of the Spirit (Luke 4:14). It was no wonder that Jesus was able to say with such confidence in the synagogue in Nazareth, 'The Spirit of the Lord is on me.' It was the presence of this prophetic Spirit of revelation that enabled Jesus to 'hear' and 'see' clearly what the Father was wanting to say and do in any given situation.

The importance of having the Spirit's power is given by a fascinating image at the end of Luke's Gospel. There, in Luke 24:49, Jesus instructs his disciples to stay in Jerusalem until they have been 'clothed with power from on high'. Clothes have to be appropriate for occasions. In a formal situation only a suit will do, while for informal occasions much less is satisfactory. Scripture is plain: to do the works of Jesus the disciple must have on the clothing of the Holy Spirit.

At this point in the explorations of the St Andrew's group, they began to feel challenged by the lack of the power of the Holy Spirit in their lives. The Reverend Michael Harper was invited to the church to give two talks on what it meant to be filled with the Holy Spirit. This resulted in many people being spontaneously filled with the Spirit. It was decided to start a regular healing ministry.

Mary and I joined the staff of the church just after the healing ministry had started. At this time it was based on the model given for us in the epistle of James:

> Is any one of you sick? He should call the elders of the church to pray over him and anoint him with oil in the name of the Lord. And the prayer offered in faith will make the sick person well; the Lord will raise him up. If he has sinned, he will be forgiven. Therefore confess your sins to each other and pray for each other so that you may be healed. (James 5:14–16)

Practically we worked this out in the context of the monthly communion service. There those who were sick were invited to receive the sacrament after the other communicants. As hands were laid on them for healing in the name of Jesus, the whole congregation would quietly join in prayer. We saw results. Healing was experienced in those physical ailments where the root cause was emotional pain. The peace of Jesus was ministered to inner anxieties and tensions and, as a result, physical healing followed. However, we saw very little breakthrough in areas of cancer or other illnesses that had a purely physical origin.

In the early 1980s we moved from this original model of healing which involved the whole body of the assembled church to one that more involved anointed individuals. This was one of the results of the visit of John Wimber and his team to the church when we experienced that new visitation of the Spirit that was to become known as the Third Wave. John had seen that it was God's intention that all his people should be able to minister healing through the gifts of the Spirit and in his power. As a result, specific individuals anointed by the Spirit were given opportunities to share in the prayer ministry for the sick at the end of services.

Now prayer for healing took on another dimension. Before the ending of the worship services, the leaders allowed a prayer time for the congregation to wait on the Lord. Then members of the congregation were encouraged to share any specific revelations they might have received concerning the medical conditions of the people present. Up to 20 revelations might be given, and those to whom they applied were invited to come forward for prayer ministry, along with anyone else needing prayer. Those who responded to the words that were given out were often amazed by the accuracy of the revelations. They found this an encouragement, showing them that God knew everything about them and that he cared for them.

During the prayer time at the end of the service the main focus was on invoking the presence and power of the Holy Spirit. This involved listening for his voice and seeking to be guided by him. On one occasion, I was praying for a young mother who had swollen knees and a painful lower back that meant she was in constant pain. Only the week before she had seen a consultant, who after tests and examinations had said that he was unable to find any cause for her condition and had prescribed painkilling tablets. As I prayed, I heard the Holy Spirit tell me that the cause was grief. This indeed turned out to be the case. Two years before, she had lost her godfather, a man who had been like a father to her. At the time, the pain had been so great that she had been unable to grieve and had suppressed her emotions. Once the grief had been broken through prayer, she expressed her pain with many tears and within 20 minutes had been completely healed.

This way of dealing with sickness became the pattern in our church over the years that followed and we had seen many successes. As I lay there with my broken bones and nerves in the hospital, I went over some of the ones I had been involved with. They reassured me that God could heal today.

I remembered one meeting where I had spoken in the lounge of a public house where members of a Baptist church met on a Sunday morning. As I stood up to speak, I became aware of a woman quietly sobbing, the tears flowing down her cheeks. After the meeting, she avoided being prayed with and I took her a cup of coffee and sat down with her. As we talked, it came out that her grief was because her eight-year-old son had been killed. I assumed that it must have been a recent accident and was surprised when she said that it had occurred eight years earlier. What had happened had been truly traumatic. She had been walking on a footpath with the child when something in the gutter had caught his eye. He had stepped into the road to pick it up and been struck by a passing lorry. Death had been instantaneous. Together, we relived the tragedy. After the funeral, she had gone home, taken all his clothes and photographs and locked them away in drawers. She had not looked at any of them since the accident and she still wept every day.

I suggested that she come to the meeting in the evening and bring a photograph of her son with her. Initially she declined, saying that it was not her habit now to go out in the evening. However, when I stood to deliver my talk that evening she was in the front row and weeping again. Afterwards, when I discovered that she had in fact brought a photograph, I suggested that along with a member of my team we went to a private room. There the three of us sat around a table. The woman had not looked at the photograph but had simply placed it in her bag. I suggested that we look at it together and invited her to place it on my hand. She did this, but placed it upside down. Now I tried to encourage her to turn it the right way up. She couldn't do it and together we sat in silence for about 20 minutes. Finally, with a gentle movement of her hand, she slowly turned the photograph over. In front of us was a picture of a handsome little boy with dark, curly hair. I asked her to tell me all about him and as she did it seemed as if a bank of stored-up and unexpressed memories were let loose. It was evident that her main problem was one of denial and of not letting go of her dead son. As she talked about the boy, I suddenly had a vision in which Jesus stood at the door of the room with him, holding his hand. Behind them, the door was ajar and they seemed to be waiting to go. I realized that this would not happen until the woman said a final goodbye to him. I shared the vision with her and she replied that she was seeing the same thing. I then suggested that in her own time she should express to her son all the things that she would like to say and then say goodbye. As she said her final goodbye, the vision faded. He had gone, she said simply. After this, we broke the power of grief that had been trapped in her heart and the resulting scream was one that echoed and re-echoed through the building. Within a few days, the woman was completely healed of the pain and trauma.

I remembered too another memorable occasion when I had spoken at a meeting in Northern Ireland. This was held at Rostrevor, the home of a Christian community led by Cecil and Myrtle Kerr, and was part of a week of meetings to which people from many parts of the country had come.

I spoke at an evening meeting that started at seven and went on until nearly midnight. Just as I was about to leave, a woman approached me and asked if I would pray with her husband. I asked why they had not come for prayer earlier and was told that she had fallen on the floor under the power of the Holy Spirit. Lying there she had heard the voice of Jesus telling her to go and fetch her husband, Peter, who had been confined to a wheelchair for ten years and in continuous pain for 14. Peter was being looked after in a hospice staffed by Catholic nuns, and his wife went to the hospice and insisted that he get up and go with her to the meeting. When I asked her where her husband was now, she pointed to a slight figure curled up in a chair at the back of the building. Feeling tired, I decided that I would pray over them together, simply asking God to give them his grace. We walked towards her husband and then, halfway down the hall, I heard Jesus say to me, 'I will raise him up.' Suddenly I felt an almost physical surge of faith rise within me. I approached Peter and said simply and quietly, 'Jesus will raise you up.' As I spoke these words he slid to the floor and lay very still. Looking at him I seemed to see a deep well of pain within him. I knelt next to him on the floor and, placing my hand on his stomach, said, 'I break the power of pain in Jesus' name.' I had hardly spoken the words when he began to sob deeply and become agitated. After about 20 minutes of clearly being in great emotional pain, the agitation left him and he became still and quiet. I heard him whispering and thought I heard him praying. Finally, I suggested to his wife that she leave him on the floor until he indicated that he wanted to go, and then I made my way to bed.

The next morning my thoughts were entirely on the talk I was to give at half-past ten, and the events of the previous night had been pushed out of my mind. I arrived at the meeting and sat with my eyes closed during the opening time of worship. Suddenly I was conscious of someone tugging on the sleeve of my sweater and decided that it was Cecil Kerr indicating that it was time for me to speak. I opened my eyes and was absolutely amazed to see Peter standing in front of me. 'I am completely healed,' he said, with his arms outstretched towards me. We embraced and wept together, then I invited him and his wife to tell the gathering what had happened to them.

What had happened was this. Shortly after I had left the meeting, Peter had been taken home by his wife and put to bed in the normal way. On waking, he had felt a power like fire flowing through his body from head to feet. As he lay there, he started to flex his arms and legs and, to his joy and amazement, realized that he had been healed. He rose from his bed, took a shower, dressed himself and then went to collect his wife. Together they had walked a mile to be at the meeting. Peter said that the key moment for him was when I had said over him, 'I break the power of pain in Jesus' name.' He then told a most heartbreaking story. When he was a small child, his parents had taken his sister and emigrated to America, placing him in an orphanage. Now 57, he had never had any contact since with his family. From the orphanage he had been put in a series of homes where those with responsibility to care for him had physically and sexually abused him. As I had spoken the words of release over him, he had felt as if he were vomiting out the pain of a lifetime.

I told myself again and again in my hospital bed in New Zealand that God did heal miraculously. I had seen how he had healed others spectacularly and I believed that he could heal me. Sooner or later, I kept repeating to myself, I would be restored to full health.

Yet, as I write this, I have to say that a full and complete healing has not happened. I have had prayer for full healing at least once a week ever since returning to England, but my condition has not substantially changed. I still have the stiff neck, the lack of feeling in my hands and arms, the imperfect balance and the blurred vision. Yet I know God could have healed me instantly.

I have no easy answers as to why full healing has not happened, but I am strangely helped by the concept of the hidden, far side of the moon. One face of the moon is fixed towards earth and the other – the far side – is permanently hidden from our view. The first time human eyes gazed upon it was in December 1968 during the historic voyage of Apollo 8. I have always been fascinated by space travel and I well remember listening and watching intently, along with millions of others, as the voyage of Apollo 8 unfolded. As it was the first manned flight around the moon, involving all sorts of new equipment and technology, there were numerous risks. I particularly remember the eerie moment when the radio links to earth fell silent as the craft slid behind the moon, and how after many tense minutes of silence there was tremendous relief as the crew's voices were heard again. However, what impressed me was not so much the risk of the mission or the excitement, but the spine-tingling fact that for the first time in human history, men had set eyes on the other side of the moon. Even now, 30-odd years later, barely a dozen people have ever gazed on that vast, unfamiliar face of the moon that looks away from us.

That image of another, hidden side is something that I feel applies also to God's relations with us. Many of God's purposes for us and his dealings with us are as plain as the face of the full moon at night. We see these plainly and we concentrate on them – the areas where his purposes are plain and open and easy to understand. Yet we must not forget that there is also another side of God's dealings with us; a side that is less easy to comprehend. I know that it is still part of his loving purpose for us, but its meaning is hidden from our sight.

There is only so much that we can see and comprehend. I believe that in my ordeal in the waves, in my suffering in hospital and in my remaining problems, I have encountered something of that other, hidden side of God's dealings with me. I have come to accept that. It seems to me to be naïve to think that a loving heavenly Father God would always hand out on demand to us what we want, and would always explain his actions to us. God's ways, I remind myself again, are beyond our comprehension. In the words of Isaiah 55 again, '"For my thoughts are not your thoughts, neither are your ways my ways," declares the LORD.'

The Bible expresses such a concept. The book of Job, scholars think, may be the oldest book of the Bible. In the mouth of Eliphaz, one of Job's counsellors, we find the following words: 'Blessed is the man whom God corrects; so do not despise the discipline of the Almighty. For he wounds, but he also binds up; he injures, but his hands also heal' (Job 5:17–18).

This same truth is stated by the eighth-century BC prophet Hosea: 'Come, let us return to the LORD. He has torn us to pieces but he will heal us; he has injured us but he will bind up our wounds' (Hosea 6:1). These, and many other scriptures, make it plain that for his own good purposes, the Lord 'wounds', 'tears to pieces' and 'injures' those whom he loves. Evidently God allows and even inflicts suffering on his children. Why? The full answer has not been given us and, like the far side of the moon, remains mysterious. It does seem certain, however, that he does these things in love so that a far greater blessing can be worked out in the lives of his children.

I do not fully understand why this accident happened to me and I do not know why, as yet, I have not had full healing. Yet I do know two things. First, God has used these events for good in my life, a point I want to talk more about in a moment. Second, one day I will know why. The apostle Paul at the end of his famous chapter on love in 1 Corinthians 13 says this about the future state of the believer: 'Now we see but a poor reflection as in a mirror; then we shall see face to face. Now I know in part; then I shall know fully, even as I am fully known.' One day I will be given the answer why. One day I will be allowed to gaze on the hidden side of God's love for me.

And I can wait.

EPILOGUE

Beyond the Storm

I may not be able to say with certainty why I had my accident or why I have not been fully healed. There are, however, some things I can say confidently. In particular, I feel that I have made many discoveries through what happened to me. Some of the things I have found out are such paradoxes that if they had not happened to me, I would have found them hard to believe.

I have found the paradox that in being made weak I have been blessed. My experience in riding the storm has left me, humanly speaking, fragile and vulnerable. Yet in this I have found a new strength in Christ. The apostle Paul tells in 2 Corinthians 12 how he had been severely troubled by some mysterious affliction that he termed 'a thorn in my flesh'. Three times, we read, he pleaded with the Lord to have it taken away. Instead, Jesus told him, 'My grace is sufficient for you, my power is made perfect in weakness.' Paul ended up delighting in his weakness because of the way Jesus' power had to work in him as a result. In my case, while I would not delight in my afflictions, I can rejoice that they have led me to have a dependence on Jesus in a way I never had before. Before the accident, I was tempted to rely on myself, on my own powers and abilities. And behind that subtle and apparently innocent temptation to trust in myself lay a deadly and strangling pride. God has broken the grip of that on me. Now, before undertaking any preaching or ministry, my weakened physical condition forces me to realize that I am nothing and that I have nothing to offer except what the Lord gives me. When I stand to speak, I am often conscious of my stiff neck and the cold numbness in my hands and lower arms. I keep asking to be cleansed from my sins and constantly invite the Holy Spirit to fill me. Yet I believe that his grace is sufficient for me and his power is made perfect in my weakness.

I have found another paradox in the fact that my weakened condition has given me a new freedom in my ministry. I find this less easy to explain. Is it, I wonder, that having come so close to losing everything, I now feel that I have nothing to lose? Perhaps too it reflects the new-found realization that what I have is no longer 'my' ministry to worry about. It is God's. This has been particularly liberating in the area of prophetic ministry. In the past, I often had what I thought to be a revelation into a person's life but found it too hard to tell them. I kept quiet. Now I am bolder. I sometimes find myself walking across a room and speaking out the revelations I have received.

I have found that I have been made thankful for so many blessings. There are the obvious things to be thankful for. I am profoundly grateful to everyone who helped me in so many ways: the people at the beach, the medical staff in Palmerston North, those who visited me in hospital and the many in New Zealand and the rest of the world who supported Mary and me in prayer and in so many other ways during those difficult times. I am, of course, grateful to Mary for her great love and labours. Most of all, I am grateful to God for the privilege of being able to continue to minister in what is still a beautiful world. I am grateful too for the less obvious things. I am more aware of the beauty of nature than

I ever was. I appreciate the small, silly things in life that I always took for granted: to be able to get in and out of bed unaided, to put my own clothes on, to walk to the shops. I thank God for all these blessings, great and small.

I have found that having known God's comfort to me I want to share it with others who need comforting. God comforted me in easing pain, providing friendship and even in such apparently trivial matters as supplying rugby tickets. In the spirit of 2 Corinthians 1:4 ('For just as the sufferings of Christ overflow into our lives so also through Christ our comfort overflows . . .') this is now something that I want to share. I can far more easily identify now with those who have disabilities, the traumatized, the bed-ridden, those who have been disappointed with some expected or promised healing. I can sympathize more. I have been there.

I have found that the symptoms I still suffer are a useful spiritual reminder. Each time I become aware of the numbness in my hands and I feel the twinges of pins and needles there, I think of how Jesus underwent this – and much, much more – for my sake. Some Christians wear gold or silver crosses around their necks to remind them of what Jesus did for them. I feel that God has given me reminders in my own flesh, bones and nerves of what his Son did for me. In the Old Testament we read in Genesis 32 how Jacob, about to return to the Promised Land, wrestled all night with a mysterious stranger who turned out to be God himself. Finally, with dawn about to break, the stranger 'touched the socket of Jacob's hip so that his hip was wrenched as he wrestled with the man'. After blessing Jacob the stranger left and Jacob continued on his way limping. Jacob had a damaged hip to remind him ever after of his encounter with God. My own scars will remind me – until the time when I will need no reminding – of the moment where in the harsh waves God mysteriously met with me.

As I face the future, I find that my perspective on death has changed. I have come close to death and in the storm that almost overwhelmed me God reached out his hand and held me safe. That storm is behind me now. I know though, as we all do, that one day there will be a new blast of the storm. But I can now see clearly through the gloomy storm clouds of death to the glory beyond. I know that God will lead me through that storm too and that one bright day I will be finally and eternally with Jesus. There I will be beyond the storm for ever.

Two books by Dr Jack Deere...

Surprised by the Power of the Spirit

What caused a professor in a conservative evangelical theological college to change his mind about the Holy Spirit so radically that he had to leave?

Much more than an explanation of why one theologian came to believe in signs and wonders for today, this is a profound biblical apologetic, arguing carefully and courteously for the view that the Holy Spirit's supernatural gifts did not cease in New Testament times.

Surprised by the Voice of God

This book is written for ordinary Christians who want to hear God's voice above the clamour of everyday life. Jack Deere brings together inspiring stories from people who have learned to trust God's voice today, his own experiences in teaching and pastoral ministry, and mature biblical teaching.